THE CAREER DOCTOR

THE CAREER DOCTOR

HOW TO GET – AND KEEP –
THE JOB YOU WANT

EOGHAN MCDERMOTT

CURRACH
PRESS

First published in 2009 by
CURRACH PRESS
55A Spruce Avenue, Stillorgan Industrial Park, Blackrock, County Dublin
www.currach.ie

1 3 5 4 2

Cover by Sin É design
Origination by Currach Press
Printed in Ireland by ColourBooks, Baldoyle Industrial Estate, Dublin 13
ISBN:978-1-85607-982-2

ACKNOWLEDGEMENTS

Thanks to my family: Dan, Veronica, Emer and Carolyn, who support everything I do (whether they agree with it or not).

Thanks to all the people who contributed to the Industry View pieces. Their insights were invaluable.

Thanks to everybody in the Communications Clinic for their support, patience and good humour: Hilary Kenny, Stephanie Brady, Karla Sloyan, Ailish Smith, Karagh Fox, Ruth Hickey and Gerard Kenny.

A special thank you to my mentors since I was in college – Managing Director Anton Savage, Chairman Tom Savage and Director Terry Prone, all of the Communications Clinic. Anton took me under his wing when I was studying. He gave me advice, trained, developed, cajoled and challenged me more than UCD ever could. The three of them are second only to my family in their influence on my life. They have given me every opportunity to develop myself and my skills. They're mighty. Without the encouragement and guidance of Terry this book would never have been written.

Thanks to Andrew Mernagh for giving me the space and scope to give advice to readers.

Finally, thanks to all the clients I've met over the years. Without all their questions, challenges, quirks, problems and successes, I wouldn't have had much to write about.

For Carolyn

CONTENTS

1

WHY THIS BOOK?

If you've picked up this book and are asking yourself, 'Why should I buy this?', the answer is: because you need it.

You need it because it is stuffed, not just with good advice, but with good advice based on experience. The Careers Clinic is based on decades of experience. Our tutors have dealt with literally thousands of job-seekers, building up an understanding of every layer of the employment market that's second to none. This understanding means that our advice is practical and personal. It's this advice that has made our clients sixteen times more likely to get the job they want. Some of our clients are unemployed, some have just left university, some are looking for a promotion in their companies and some are going for chief executive positions.

As recently as 2008, all a graduate had to do was fire their CV off to a couple of recruitment companies and wait for the offers to come in. It's not like that any more. The employment scene has done a 180-degree turn in just twelve months. Now it's a buyer's market, with more and more people chasing fewer and fewer jobs.

The Career Doctor is the book you need if:

- You've been unemployed since leaving school or graduating from college.
- You're trying to return to the workforce because things have got tight with the recession.
- You've been fired or made redundant.
- You've taken early severance, the 'golden handshake', but you don't figure on spending twenty-five years watching morning TV.
- You're bored out of your mind in your present job.
- You set up your own business in the good times. Now it has gone down the Swanee and you need a job.
- You've seen an advertisement for a position or been head-hunted for a job you really want.

If your situation is even a little like any of the above, you must buy this book. If you follow the detailed plans laid out in the following pages, you will radically improve your chances of getting the job you want. I say this with total confidence because I see it work every single day. My colleagues and I help people to get their CVs, covering letters, application forms, their approach and their interview skills right. And – just as important – as the Head of the Careers Clinic, I don't commission advertising to promote it. I don't need to. We're lucky enough to get all our work through word-of-mouth. People who have succeeded in a difficult job-seeking situation tell other people. Husbands send us their wives, mothers their sons. We know what we're at – and you hold a good chunk of our wisdom in your hand when you hold this book.

We know, for example, that the first thing you have to do,

when you go looking for a job, is to regard job-seeking as a full-time project. You're not between jobs. You're completely engaged in a vital task. It might take six days, six weeks or six months but for that period of time you are fully employed in self-marketing. You don't get paid for this marketing project, but if you do it right you'll have no long-term money problems. (Plus, you might even enjoy it, as opposed to experiencing job-seeking as a highly stressful interruption to your real life.)

This unpaid marketing project is arguably the most interesting job you'll ever have. You will master more practical skills faster than at any time in your educational or professional life and gain more solidly-based confidence in yourself. These are the job specifications for the marketing project:

- Eight-hour day, five days a week
- Dress code
- Research
- Self-examination
- Cold calling
- Writing of CVs and covering letter
- Delivery of interview

In this marketing project you are going to be selling a one-off unique product, rather than something coming off an assembly line. We're not talking yellow-pack here, we're talking about a fascinating individual about whom you have huge understanding and knowledge.

When people are out of work and searching for a job, managing time becomes vital. Time can be a liability for unemployed people when they end up sleeping more than they would if they had a job. They sleep more because they have nowhere to be at a particular time on any given day. But they also sleep more because they get depressed. Being unemployed is not a happy experience. It leads to eating more, drinking more, watching TV more, spending more time surfing the Net. Now sleeping longer than usual is OK if you're unemployed, but if you're unemployed and actively determined to get a job, you should be sleeping less because you've a lot of work to do and a short time in which to do it. And on a practical level, a sleep pattern that starts an hour after midnight and lasts until midday or later is going to be difficult to break.

One of the most successful clients I've worked with was unexpectedly let go from a job he had assumed he would hold for life. Although he was devastated, his hobby came to his rescue. His hobby was reading about the Holocaust. You might not think this would be helpful to someone who had lost their job but it was, in fact, enormously helpful. Because one of the things he picked up about concentration-camp inmates was a tiny insight about survival. The inmates who saved a little of their water ration every day and used it to do a rudimentary wash tended to survive, whereas the inmates who abandoned all concern for self-presentation and simply drank the water tended to die. This man decided to learn from his Holocaust library. During the many months of his unemployment, he got up early, shaved every day and wore clean and smart clothes. He did this because he felt he needed to keep his own morale up.

'I don't want to develop downwardly mobile habits in myself,' was the way he put it.

Getting a job should become your number one focus and

project. Treat it like a full-time job. You'll have an eight-hour day in front of you. Most job-seekers waste a lot of time on worrying about getting a job, but don't spend time systematically on the tasks that, properly completed, will guarantee them the job.

Break down your day and develop a timetable of activities on a spreadsheet on your computer or on a sheet of paper. Don't cheat yourself by drifting into time-wasting pursuits. The objective of the form is to help you to allocate time each day to the various challenges you are going to tackle in preparing to sell yourself in the jobs market. On the spreadsheet you should note how much time you plan to spend on these tasks:

- Research (reading advertisements, searching the internet)
- Preparation of your CV and covering letters
- Meeting people within your network

The following chapters in this book will help you with these tasks.

2

Always Look on the Bright Side of Life...

Job hunting involves a lot of rejection. A giant longitudinal study in Germany (lasting for twenty years or more), looking at the impact of life events across a huge chunk of population, has found that losing a job is the single most negative event a person can experience. The study found that not only does losing a job upset people and their families at the time, it causes lasting damage. While it's easy for other people to say 'Nobody died,' the reality is that, for the person who has lost the job, the experience is remarkably close to a bereavement, especially if their identity is tightly wound up with the responsibilities, title and prestige of that job. It can feel like a little death and it almost always feels like a public reproach: if you had done something better, this wouldn't have happened to you.

Because the recession that began in 2008 is the first Irish recession that hit highly qualified people, like architects, accountants and lawyers as well as carpenters and plumbers, the reassurance of being insulated by education has been unexpectedly stripped away. This, in turn, makes professional people who have lost their jobs less optimistic: if, having studied hard and gained all these qualifications, I still find myself laid off, what can I do, what more can I study in order to get a new job other than one flipping burgers in McDonald's?

The first and most important thing to do, if you find yourself in this unwelcome position, is to get real and get realistic. Every day you spend in depressed bafflement is a day that damages you, your family and those close to you. Every time you rail against the unfairness of what has happened to you, you become less in control of your destiny, more at the mercy of external circumstances.

Try not to take this rejection personally. In the past, if you lost your job, it might have been an indictment of you, personally. When you lose your job in a massive economic down-swing, it's quite different. It isn't your fault. But neither is it the end of the world. Other jobs will come along and there's a good chance that you may actually gain from the experience. This will happen only if you decide what gains are possible. You may decide to get fit, to run with your dog every day, having postponed it when you were too busy to take care of yourself or the dog. You may decide to read a number of books you've always meant to read. You may do some voluntary work to keep yourself engaged with people whose problems (you will quickly learn) are a lot worse than those affecting you. You may decide to talk to some company about giving them your services for free for three months to gain work experience and make sure your CV doesn't develop a black hole.

And, of course, you will have a new job anyway. The 'Getting Myself a Job' job. It's going to take up a good deal of your time and entail a fair amount of disappointment. Getting a job is a series of 'nos' followed by a single 'yes': but you only need the one yes. To be successful you must learn how to cope with rejection and not take it personally.

There's a good chance, as you read this, that you're saying 'Easy for him to say...' If you're saying this, you probably feel that the recession has hit you worse than most other people and you resent anybody who's been less punished than you. Don't waste your time on that kind of self-positioning. Because sinking into that mood is the single worst thing you can do for yourself. It will make you more depressed and that depression will show. Every day I meet clients in my Careers Clinic who have painted themselves into a depressed corner and who, if they went for a job interview the day I meet them, would fail because of the cloud of despondency surrounding them. Others, who have similarly lost their jobs, manage to be a little more positive. Although they don't know it, that subtle difference in mood radically improves their chance of getting a job when they go for interview. Being resilient and optimistic is important for success in any economic climate and critical in a recession.

Employers and recruiters do not select people for jobs because the people have been hard done by. They may be altruistic and public-spirited but they're not in the business of charity. (Even the ones who are in the charity business want someone who can deliver on the requirements of the job speedily and cheerfully; not someone dragging themselves around like Mrs Gummidge, the character in Charles Dickens' *David Copperfield*, who burst into tears when the fire smoked and when it was pointed out to her that everybody in the room was equally inconvenienced said that she felt it more.)

Never forget that potential employers, consciously or unconsciously, are out to avoid disaster in their new hires and to add to the happiness and productivity in their business with every new hire. Jerry Kennelly, the photographer who sold his visual archive to Getty Images for more than a hundred million Euro and immediately began to set up new businesses in Tralee, County Kerry, puts it very simply when he addresses conferences on HR and Recruitment issues: 'Don't hire gobshites' reads one of his PowerPoint slides. He hammers it hard: hiring a gobshite means endless pointless hours devoted to advice, encouragement and training to try to move that person from being a gobshite into being a positive contributor to the business. Kennelly maintains that it's possible to spot who, among potential new recruits, will be the gobshite and who will be the contributor, if recruiters pay enough attention at the interview stage.

David Maister, the English consultant who has written some excellent books about the whole process of management consultancy, puts a more positive cast on the same reality. He talks about the importance of hiring 'the people with the shining eyes'. Meeting a person with 'shining eyes' lights up everybody's day. Getting the chance to work with a 'shining eyes' person is a gift – in a meeting, an interview or even on the phone, they light up others' days. They have energy, enthusiasm and the get-up-and-go to keep chipping away until they succeed.

One of the most interesting chunks of supportive evidence for what I'm saying comes from the work of an American professor of psychology named Martin Seligman. Seligman has developed a concept called 'learned optimism'. It refers to the acknowledgement people make when confronted with failure or setbacks. He has rigorously researched this topic for more than thirty years and has found that optimism and resilience are vital components to predicting high achievers. His research has shown that optimists tend to make specific, temporary, external causal acknowledgments while pessimists make global, permanent, internal ones. He discovered that people are consistent in interpreting events (good or bad) in their lives. The way people explain these events, Seligman says, can predict and determine their future. It comes down, pretty much, to the moaners who blame external factors or attribute the outcomes of events to forces beyond their control (we all know the people who always say, 'It was someone else's fault') and who aren't as likely to succeed as those who believe that they're masters of their own fate. Seligman's research reveals whether or not a person will become defeated by a setback and give up or overcome it and keep fighting. You need to keep this in mind. When hunting for a job and going to interviews and not succeeding, don't lose faith. Keep working at it, ask for feedback on how you could improve, apply it and you will triumph.

In the course of his research Seligman convinced insurance giants, MetLife, to launch a highly original pilot programme to hire new recruits. Management's best predictor of success, Seligman argued, is the candidate's level of optimism. MetLife managers were unsure but intrigued. Seligman, sure of his theory, said to MetLife that if the salesmen he picked didn't outsell the others he'd pay them and if they did, MetLife would pay them. Seligman and his colleagues found that new salesmen who were optimists sold 37 per cent more insurance in their first two years than the pessimists. When the company hired a special group of individuals who scored high on optimism but failed the normal screening, they outsold the pessimists by 21 per cent in their first year and by

57 per cent in the second year. They even outsold the average agent by 27 per cent.

Seligman's research shows the incredible impact that optimism has on achievement and well-being. For example, he studied a cohort of ninety-nine Harvard University graduates who were veterans of the Second World War and had physical examinations every five years after they graduated. The men who were optimists at twenty-five were significantly healthier at sixty-five than the pessimists. In sport, he analysed members of several professional baseball teams and found that optimists regularly surpassed expectations.

A colleague of mine, Enda McNulty (All-Ireland football winner with Armagh in 2002 and Managing Director of Motiv8), is an expert on motivation and he believes that mental toughness or resilience is essential 'technology' at the highest level in sport and life across the globe:

> Athletes and players like Michael Jordan, Rafael Nadal and Michael Phelps have developed extraordinary mental toughness. 'Corporate athletes' now realise that in order to survive and thrive in the eye of this economic storm they must develop their 'mental armoury' so they have the same toughness and resilience as Michael Jordan or Bernard Dunne or Katy Taylor.
>
> Mental toughness can be developed in much the same way as we can develop our communication skills or our physical fitness: by conditioning a new pattern. Michael Jordan did not become extremely mentally tough and cool under pressure by doing one session. It takes

the same effort, intensity, focus and coaching to improve your mental toughness as to improve your physical fitness. Optimism and positivity are essential mental kit to enable us to fend off the ferocious storm that rages in the economy. Any person who reads newspapers or watches news channels or who simply listens to their peers is likely to be exposed to a barrage of negativity. Successful sports people, successful individuals and successful teams in business and sport are much more likely to be optimistic about their chances of survival and success.

One way to be more positive is to try not to moan or complain for a week, a fortnight or a month. Maxwell Maltz, author of the book *Psycho Cybernetics*, claims that it takes twenty-one days to form a habit. Ask your friends, family and colleagues to help you. If they catch you moaning, you have to give them €2. Simply saying, 'I'm not going to moan any more,' isn't going to change your behaviour. If you keep trying, eventually your behaviour will begin to change. What makes it difficult is that behavioural change doesn't happen as a result of a single decision. It happens as a result of a single decision backed up by (at worst) daily and (at best) hourly self-reminders and practice. If you're planning to become a more positive person, you have to start by identifying what's wrong with your current view (too much moaning or complaining perhaps), work out how you're going to measure how much you move away from that bad pattern and then concentrate on building a whole new habit of positive attention.

In the short term, if you hammer away at it, your positivity will improve. In the long term, if you keep at it, your character may eventually improve, so that people describe you as 'a very positive person'.

Behavioural resolutions are more about deliverable, measurable small improvements than they are about great overarching visions of personal change. This means that you must continue to perform the new behaviour for twenty-one days (or as long as it takes) until performance of the new behaviour is automatic. It also means quelling that little voice within yourself that says, 'I'm never going to get this right.' Most of us had that little voice rabbiting at us when we were learning to drive and smoothly letting out the clutch while depressing the accelerator seemed beyond us. But within a matter of weeks, the technique had become a habit we didn't need to think about.

Skills-building was described by psychologist Abraham Maslow as going through four phases. Stage one he called 'unconscious incompetence'. This simply means that we are not aware that we need to work on a skill. Stage two is 'conscious incompetence'. At this stage we have identified what we need to work on. Stage three is 'conscious competence', the stage in which we work and practise our skill. Finally comes Stage four: 'unconscious competence'. This happens after practising and working on the skill every day. We don't have to think about doing it. It comes naturally and is internalised.

According to Martin Seligman, in order to be a success in business, your company should exhibit a 5:1 ratio of positives to negatives. A successful individual should display a ratio of 4:1. At the moment the likelihood is that you are exposed to a 10:1 ratio of negative to positive. Remember the old maxim: 'Negative information in...negative information and results out.' Put simply, if we feed our minds with negative thoughts, negative images and negative feelings, in addition to becoming pessimistic there is a strong probability that we will produce a negative outcome.

In the job hunt you're going to need to be persistent. Don't let the knocks get you down. Pessimists give up.

'I can't take this rejection,' they decide. 'Nobody is hiring. Things are going to get worse. The economy is never going to recover. I'm off to Oz.'

In contrast, Seligman found (even in children) that optimists keep trying something until they master it. And these tendencies can last a lifetime.

'It's not reality itself that's the problem,' Seligman concludes. 'We all suffer tragic realities; how you see reality is the difference.' We all interpret events and develop a point of view about life, which in turn colours the way we approach the future. In job-searching terms, pessimists need a kick-start to realise that they can, with hard work and perseverance, succeed in the job hunt.

What you see depends on where you stand. You need to stand in the shoes of the prospective employer. If you do that, you will quickly appreciate just how much more welcome is a call from or an interview with a bright-eyed enthusiastic go-getter who is convinced they could contribute to the success of the business, as opposed to a draggy self-absorbed pessimist. Even if the company doesn't, right now, have a job for the person with the shining eyes, they will keep them in mind or refer them on to someone else.

3

The Cull – What Disqualifies You and How to Avoid It

For the foreseeable future, the employment situation is going to be a buyer's market. We've seen McDonald's being inundated with CVs for jobs when a new franchise opened and learned, with dismay, that the bulk of the applicants for the hamburger-grilling jobs were lawyers and accountants, spun loose from their previous places of employment. Until recently, the top law and accountancy partnerships were in fierce competition every year, producing elaborate glossy brochures in an effort to attract the cream of the graduate crop. In addition to the graduate recruitment market, such firms set out to persuade suitably qualified members of the Irish diaspora to come back home and welcomed 'New Irish' job applicants.

Now, the tide is flowing in the other direction, with some of these premium employers cutting staff, sometimes in grievously large numbers because they have no choice. As a result, every one of those law and accountancy firms will be inundated, this year and for several years to come, with applications for their graduate positions – if they still have graduate positions.

In a buyer's market, the first thing buyers do is seek a method of simplifying their task. So they look through the cover letters, application forms and CVs for the disqualifiers, the factors that allow them to dump this particular applicant without reading further and without interviewing him or her. Don't bother applying to one of the bigger firms if you know you lack one of the key qualifiers they require. You're just wasting your time. Whereas a smaller firm may be attracted by some peripheral qualification you have or by the cleverness of your cover letter or the impressiveness of your referees, the computer-cull in the larger firms won't even register such special pleading so it makes no sense to employ it.

The truly sad thing is that job applicants sometimes assist the cull by gratuitously providing potential employers with data detrimental to themselves. That happens, for instance, when you have a commitment to social networking that outweighs your long-term commitment to having a great career. Some large firms now automatically Google applicants and check what's on the web about them. This means you need to be careful with Bebo, Facebook, MySpace and Twitter.

As the Career Doctor, I have to replicate the process an employer goes through before they interview a job applicant so that I can give every client the most exhaustive and realistic preparation they could get anywhere – which means that every CV that arrives on my desk gets a quick Google. For example, a young guy came in for a job interview session a few months ago and was excellent. We finished the interview assessment; I finalised the DVD we had recorded so he could take it with him and do some more work at home.

'What about your Bebo page?' I asked him casually.

'What about it?'

'Lot of comments on it that any potential employer would find inappropriate – unless you want to be a bouncer in a lap-dancing club.'

Silence.

'Some of the pictures too,' I said. 'More or less show you engaging in…"lewd conduct".'

If he was serious about his job hunt, he needed either to delete his profile or do sweeping edits on it, although even the sweeping edits may not be enough. There should be a warning on each of these social networking sites: 'What you post on these sites may be used against you in a recruitment process.'

INDUSTRY VIEW

Krishna De is an award-winning brand engagement and digital marketing author, mentor and commentator. She believes social networks can be a positive thing for career development, but people need to be very careful:

> There has been a rapid increase in the popularity of social networking sites as a way to connect and build relationships with past colleagues, friends and potential contacts. The Neilson Global Faces and Networked Places report reported that across the globe in 2008, activity in 'Member Communities' now accounts for one in every eleven minutes spent online (in the UK it's one in every six minutes). One of the biggest mistakes people make when joining a community online is not reviewing and refining the privacy settings for their profile. Some social

networks are completely open, so that whatever you post can be seen by everyone else in the community and may even be indexed online. An example of that would be IGOpeople.com, the Irish social network for professionals and businesses. This means that whatever you post online can be found in the search engines.

Many social networks require you to establish your privacy settings. There is a benefit of allowing your profile to be available for others to find – many people today search online for us by name, not just the company we work for. Being digitally distinctive is becoming more important if we want to stand out in a crowded marketplace. But make sure that when people search for you online the content they find is relevant and related to how you want to be known professionally. If in doubt, don't post photographs, videos or content to the web that you would not be happy to be found by your current or a potential employer or you would not want to appear on the front page of the national newspapers. When you set up your profile online, where possible, use your name across all social networks in a consistent way which will help people find you. Try to avoid using numbers in your profile name as that will make it harder for people to remember how to find you. Adding a professional photograph will also enhance your profile.

As you begin to post content to your profile

online, take the time to consider what you want to be remembered for in relation to your personal brand (in other words, your reputation). If you are a marketing manager, for example, can you share articles and insights or even recommendations for books or events that are relevant to your expertise, which will act as a reminder for people and showcase that you are keeping your own skills and professional development up to-date. And remember to use 'key words' in your profile online – as the social network is online, people will be able to search for you using words that represent your profession or job title.

Many profiles allow you to write a short summary: make sure that your summary passes the ten-second test so that when someone reads it they can quickly understand what you do. Your profile must clearly project who you are and your expertise, even if someone were to scan it briefly. Networking is essentially about building relationships with others and those people who are the most successful in developing a network have a mindset of 'how to help their network'. In other words, giving to their network before asking for help for themselves. Taking time to connect with the key people in your network and where you can assist them, perhaps, connecting them to people you know or answering questions they may have that you are able to help them with is a great way of nurturing your network and will help you to recession-proof your career.

Earlier in this chapter, I touched on the fact that some of the more high-powered legal and accountancy firms have electronic 'cull' programmes which effectively remove from consideration any candidate whose academic qualifications fall below a particular level.

They're not alone in this. Recruitment companies now have software on their systems that cut out people who don't meet certain educational requirements. If you run up against a disqualifier, it doesn't matter if your CV is printed on gold-leaf paper, perfumed with the tears of angels and bound in leather; nor does it matter that you can dazzle in the interview: you're dead.

It may not seem fair to you, if you know you can do the job better than some of your highly-qualified peers, but the fact is that having a qualification on your CV gives a prospective employer some reassurance that at least you have the ability to study, retain and apply information. For certain careers a degree is an absolute and immutable requirement. (And before you rail against it, get real. Do you want someone doing neurosurgery on you who has done only 'sit by Nellie' observation, or do you want a highly qualified neurosurgeon?)

Before you invest pointless time in a CV that may go unread, face up to the most frequent disqualifiers:

UNDER-QUALIFIED/UNDER-EDUCATED

The lack of a degree (or lack of an appropriate degree) is the most frequently applied disqualifier. More and more job specs are looking for a master's degree. Whereas in the past a bachelor's degree was sufficient, more companies are now looking for the MA after the name. Much the same factor is coming into play within specific sectors. For example, in law, until relatively recently, a basic law degree was usually enough to get you into a big law firm. You would then be expected to sit your FE1s during your first year or two. Now the big firms rarely offer a graduate position to someone who hasn't at least started sitting (and passing) them.

In the 1980s, going to university and getting a BA was the be-all and end-all. Now I'd question whether a graduate qualification is sufficient any more. Many of my clients in their late twenties and early thirties have a master's degree or higher, not necessarily acquired immediately after their primary degree. Some of them went for a job based on their first qualification and saw that they needed more education to make progress in their chosen career. Many companies now support their graduate intake to improve their skills and qualifications, from which the company will benefit. In some cases, people find they need to switch tracks away from their original choice if it turns out not to be as good a match for their career ambitions as they thought. The best way to be considered for a change of role may be to get a different qualification; this is made easier if you have a basic degree in the first place. (Most, if not all, postgraduate courses require a third-level qualification.) In a more competitive jobs market every extra advantage you can summon helps. You'd be wise to consider how you might get an extra qualification, the one that one is best suited to your strengths and abilities and to current skills shortages.

Solution:
Get the degree, master's degree or industry qualifications. If you want to aim high, in career terms, go back to college. Get

the extra level of qualification. Or resign yourself either to an inferior job or a longer wait.

INEXPERIENCED
You have your degree and it's a good one. But you have never worked. For many companies, those two factors add up to a disqualifier. They want highly qualified people who have been 'broken in' to the workings of industry. For example, they don't want bright marketing graduates who are full of high-flown theory and who have little grasp of the sober realities of day-to-day work. This area is a hobby-horse of mine. I believe that all graduates need to have work experience under their belt. I'm a product of a work experience programme. It gave me an opportunity to understand business, show the company that I was good, build relationships with the people in there and ultimately build a career. Irish universities – in particular DCU – have well-established links with companies that enable their students to get experience.

Some individual students ferret out work experience for themselves. One of the Communications Clinic's most reliable technicians, who is in the process of developing into a consultant, is a Trinity College student who – while he enjoys studying, college sport/social life and does well in exams – has his eye, already, on his employability. None of us can quite remember when he started to hang around our place, but every one of us would – right now – give him a reference as one of the fastest learners and most reliable professionals we know. How could he ever have got to that point without work experience?

Our TCD student copped on to the reality that degrees are now a given and that the key way to differentiate yourself, when it comes to competing for a job, is through your work experience. If you're still in college, you might usefully follow his example and get work experience while you're studying. Even a day a week can be useful. For example, if you're studying law, getting some work in a legal firm would be of great value to you and prospective employers. While you're studying it gives you an opportunity to see the application of the theory first hand. It also gives you experience of a work environment and the things that will be expected of you. The work experience (if you do well) gives you an in to the company and also work experience to point to in future interviews. It shows your interest in the industry too and proves that you've practically come out of the womb wanting to work in law.

Solution
Get experience. Without documented experience of the real workplace, you're like a one-legged tap dancer.

COMING FROM THE WRONG FIELD
You're qualified as an architect and you want to get into communications consultancy. Employer's reaction? 'Gimme a break!' Or you've been working as a teacher and you want to get into theatre management. To the potential employer you're a liability in the short-term even if you prove to be a long-term asset.

Solution
Do a course. Do some freelancing. Do some networking. Even better: give up your summer holidays and get some unpaid experience somewhere.

THEY DON'T NEED/CAN'T AFFORD YOU

You're qualified, competent and might be an asset to the company you're aiming for. But they're not advertising for recruits and they don't want any. Their business plan doesn't include taking on any new people. Not you. Not anybody.

Solution

The only way to infiltrate companies such as this is to come up with a plan which allows them to explore a new market at no cost. Prove to them that you're capable of achieving this kind of development and that you're prepared to contribute time for free. If they buy into your concept, then all you have to demonstrate is that you're indispensable and that they have to have you. Easy peasy. Seriously, though. Be wary of knocking on the door of a company that clearly is not hiring unless you're sure you've something to offer which will make them reconsider their decision.

YOU DON'T SEEM RESPONSIBLE ENOUGH

I'm currently meeting a number of job-seeking clients who decided to go to Australia or on a world tour for a couple of years after they graduated. They're having difficulty in the recruitment game because some employers – whether they say it out loud or just think it – look askance at the group known informally as the 'Ozzie AWOLs': the folk who need a couple of years (sometimes at their parents' expense) to 'find themselves' and who typically do much of the searching on beaches with surfable waves.

If you're in this group, put yourself in the shoes of the employer and work out what you gained from your year (or more than a year) off that can be of relevance to them. They do not care that you are a more fulfilled and happy bunny. All any employer cares about in the current climate, is how contributory a bunny you will be to their hutch. Here are the two questions they always have, in the back of their minds, about 'Ozzie AWOLs':

1. Is this guy/dame so cosseted by their parents that they've no real sense of how tough business actually is?
2. If this person took off for a year or more to 'find themselves', what are the chances they might feel another search for self coming on and abandon this job a few months down the line if I employ them?

YOU WANT TO MOVE BETWEEN SECTORS

A trend at the moment is that people are moving from the private sector into teaching, for instance. Science teachers have been in demand, particularly in the areas of physics and chemistry. One client of mine, who worked as a financial adviser, left one of the major banks to go and teach business and maths. He found teaching much more rewarding and challenging. He enjoyed watching his students develop, learn and discover new things with his help. The shorter hours and three months of summer holidays also gave him more freedom to do the things he wanted to do and spend more time with his family. The move did, however, mean that he had less money to spend. But a number of studies have proven that, once you have enough of an income to cover your basic needs, increases in salary have a limited effect on happiness.

Solution

If you're earning a packet in a job which pays you highly but leaves you feeling unfulfilled, don't procrastinate: take a chance, grab a bit of chalk and get teaching (or whatever your heart's desire may be). No matter how well paid you are, if you're not happy, take a drop in salary and go to what turns you on. But – and this is an important caveat – be prepared for the doubtful expression on the part of a public-sector recruiter and make sure that recruiter understands:

- The extra benefits you bring to the new job
- The trend towards mobility between the private and the public sector
- Your level of commitment to the job you're seeking, which is demonstrated by your willingness to lose money as a consequence.

YOUR PATTERN OF STUDYING SHOWS THAT YOU DITHER

In response to my Career Doctor column, I constantly receive questions from Leaving Cert students or their parents looking for advice around the area of CAO choices. If a student subsequently visits my Clinic, the end result is – at the very least – greater clarity and less waste of time because I help the student fill out the CAO in a strategic way. Meaning? Meaning that choosing medicine as a course implies that's the career you're after. If subsequent CAO choices don't allow you to migrate back to this option you need to decide whether you want to opt for a different career. If your heart is set on medicine that won't be an option. Every now and then, I meet a client who has gone through an enormously demanding university course only to come to the conclusion, in their mid or late twenties, that they don't want to embark on the career on which the course was predicated. They're then faced with the task of persuading a potential employer to give them a job for which they're not qualified, on the basis that they at least have a high level qualification in a different area. Alternatively they have to embark on another university course which will a) put them on the jobs market much later in the age cycle and b) suggest to a potential employer that they may be one of nature's ditherers.

Solution

If you're in your mid or late twenties before you qualify for the job you really want, you must position yourself as doubly qualified and doubly committed to your career because of embarking on it so late. If you're in your Leaving Cert year, think long and hard about opting for a course, rather than a career. Don't go for what your points qualify you to go for if the degree at the end of the course will only qualify you for something you really, really don't hunger to do for the rest of your life, or at least for a good portion of your working life.

4

CHANGING CAREERS

In 2004 a very successful clarinettist living in Dublin was earning big money (around €60,000 per year), had lots of work and was likely to have no shortage of it in the future. She could play. She could teach. She could organise gigs. She could network.

The only thing missing was challenge. Ruth Hickey woke up one morning and asked herself, 'Is this it?' She loved playing but had done most of the great gigs any clarinettist could hope to do. She could, of course, stick with it, earn a pretty penny, but be bored. Or jump into the unknown. She tried a couple of training courses which convinced her that a jump into the unknown might be a very good thing. One of them gave her an insight into a PR company that looked interesting. She offered herself to them. They told her they had no jobs. She refused to go away, presenting herself as an extra pair of hands if they ever needed her. She eventually left her €60k a year job as a leading clarinettist for an €18k gig as a PR junior in that company.

It was a massive decision to make, but she did it without fear and never looked back. She had most of the skills the job required – communication, organisation, teamwork and ability to meet deadlines and deal with pressure. She knew precisely the skills she didn't have and set out to develop them. She had the desire to do detailed work and achieve tangible outcomes and she was prepared to take a chance on her own talent and on the company. Ruth is now one of the best PR executives in Ireland. I know, because her section of the Communications Clinic has from a standing start in 2008 become one of the most successful operations of its kind in this country and she (along with her colleagues Gerard Kenny, Ailish Smith and Karagh Fox) is key to that success. When she did a project for the Road Safety Authority, the Chairman of the RSA dubbed her 'Ruthless' Hickey because she would always insist on getting precisely the photograph of him she knew the following day's newspapers would find interesting.

Ruth is one of the people who didn't just change jobs, she changed careers. She did it in her mid-twenties; other people do it in their twenties, then do it again in their thirties. My Career Clinic is inundated with calls and emails asking for advice on how to change careers. The requests come from people who have lost their jobs or who are fed up with their jobs, or from people who just fancy a bit of a change. If you fall into the bracket of having lost your job, you're lucky. You mightn't currently believe you're lucky, but you are. The reason you're lucky is that you will have an unequalled drive and desire to get a job and you will succeed. With that feral desire you will be hardworking, dedicated and resilient. But the best part is that you have been handed the opportunity to change course if you want to: to look at what you've been doing, look at what you might be doing and decide that the direction in which you now want to go bears no relation to the career path you always thought you'd tread.

People often ask if there is a best age at which to change jobs or careers. It might be helpful if I said, 'Yes', but the reality is that career-change can happen successfully at any time. Grandma Moses, one of America's most famous painters, never lifted a paintbrush until her extreme old age.

You shouldn't change jobs or careers just for the hell of it, or because you have some sort of vague feeling that you need an extra angle on your CV. But if an opportunity appears out of left field which you know in your gut is what you've always wanted to do, or if you find yourself yearning for something other than what you're currently doing, don't confine yourself to the rail tracks you're already on.

Cast your bread on the waters and, whilst you may be scared, you won't be bored. Does that matter? Of course it does.

Boredom is a lot more than an irritated response to routine. Clinical depression, alcoholism, drug abuse and major vehicle crashes have been attributed, in whole or in part, to boredom. One British study suggests that more than half of the workforce find their job pretty consistently boring. Nobody enjoys a boring job. But, according to psychiatrist Raj Persaud, boredom can have serious health implications. He wrote in his book *Staying Sane*:

> Medical research has found bored workers have three to five times the incidence of cardiovascular disease, four to seven times the incidence of neurological disorders, twice the incidence of gastrointestinal disorders, two to three times the incidence of musculoskeletal disorders and were absent for medical reasons three to five times as

often as their non-bored colleagues. As many as 60 per cent of Swedish mill workers doing one particular boring task received treatment for peptic ulcers.

The moral would appear to be that you should not spend your life doing a boring job, vaguely hoping the perfect job will come along while never taking a risk and ultimately never moving.

'Twenty years from now you will be more disappointed by the things you didn't do than by the ones you did,' said Mark Twain, who himself threw up a good job to become a writer. 'So throw off the bowlines. Sail away from the safe harbour. Catch the trade winds in your sails. Explore. Dream. Discover.'

Leave when you're ready to go but don't wait until it becomes the thing you never did.

If you are thinking of changing careers there is a number of things you need to look at:

1. Are qualifications needed?
2. What skills are needed
3. What experience is needed?

The answer to the qualifications question is fairly obvious – get the required one. This can cost time and money you may not believe you have, but if you really want to work in that field, you gotta do what you gotta do. For example, if you've been working as a nail technician you can't become a dental assistant without getting the relevant qualifications in the area.

If you don't need a new qualification, you should ask yourself: 'Do I have the skills or competences required to do the job?' For example, if you have been working in sales for the past ten years but would like to move into training, you've already started your development for career change. If you're any good at sales you've got a swathe of useful and applicable skills – communication, listening and an ability to build strong relationships quickly. So your next step is to decide what kind of training you want to do and for whom. One route is to apply to a specialist training company. Or there may be a training department in your current company that you could investigate joining. You can locate many different train-the-trainer courses by searching on the internet. Having one of these under your belt would do no harm. As with changing any job, you need to tailor your CV to the requirements of the new job, research the key players in the market, figure out what you have to offer them (as a salesperson that one shouldn't be a problem) and get working on it.

If you're bored in your job and want a career change, the two questions you need to ask yourself are:

- Why am I bored?
- Will I be able to afford to take a pay cut?

The second question is important because if you go into something new, you're not going to be starting at the same seniority level as in your current position. If you're well paid and important to your company, there must be a way to challenge yourself. Ever think of asking your boss, 'Hey Mick, I'm bored out of my skull, any chance of something new being thrown my way?'

That's normally a good start. If that fails then you get drastic. One of my clients is a man worth nearly €200 million who started with nothing. I asked him the obvious 'secret of his success' question. His answer stunned me: debt. He told me that every time he got his head above water, he invested himself straight back into hock and started paddling frantically. Not many people can handle that kind of constant stress. But sometimes it's a useful catalyst to get you past your biggest risk – stasis – waiting for 'something to change' or 'something to come along'. If your boss doesn't respond to your request for more challenge, set a date in your head for departure and stick to it. Research shows that once you start earning about €40,000, your salary makes little impact on your happiness. So get ready to jump in above your head. And paddle hard.

If it's experience you need, get it. Use your network, call the business cold (See Chapter 5) or beg. Even if you've been laid off and decide to go travelling, try to find some relevant work experience along the way. More and more clients come in to meet me after they've been away travelling and complain that they can't get a job in their area of choice. The common theme for all of them is that they went away for a year and worked, but worked in a job that didn't add anything to their CV. They headed off to Australia for the year saying, 'I'm not getting a real job.' But they should. For a couple of reasons: they won't have a gap in their CV; a real job will engage their brain; they develop themselves and they will have practical experience they can draw on in the job interview process and in the role when they get back home. For example, if you came back from your travels looking to work in communications, you'd find it a great deal more beneficial to have had experience in an advertisement agency than in a bar.

If you're daft enough to want to go into banking, start researching the market. See what banks, if any, are hiring and in which areas they are hiring. Your research should include your network of contacts. Do they know of any people about to move sideways in their organisation or anyone who has recently left and into whose shoes you could fit to solve a problem for the management. Use the internet, your contacts diary, your ears, to find out if there is anything. After that, the same rules of job-hunting apply as laid out in previous chapters. Get your CV up to scratch and make sure everything in it is relevant, illustrative of success and correct…even a whiff of a typo means it will get the bin. If you are called for interview, you're first of all blessed and secondly in a great position. They obviously think you're worth a look, so do yourself justice. Prepare yourself. Gather up examples that will show that you have done the job and will do it for them in the future. Finally, I'm sure you have developed transferable skills in your work life this far: teamwork, communication and the ability to meet deadlines. These can be used in all jobs.

INDUSTRY VIEW
Denis O'Flynn, HR Director with Irish Distillers, identifies skills that he looks for in all candidates:

> There are four or five traits that I am always looking for. I would describe them as inherent in the person as against learned. I see the ability to communicate as a big one and the ability to communicate in a way that's appropriate to the occasion as most important of all – what I mean

by that is the capacity to give the same message to a number of different audiences so they all understand it.

The second one is actually what I call educated risk-taking. That is really the ability to make a decision based on the best information available and to stick by that decision. I have seen people make decisions just because they are there. The important thing is to make an educated decision. And if you have made it and you have the best information, you don't regret that decision. You stick with it and you work through it.

The third is delegation. I regard the inability to delegate as the biggest inhibitor to promotion of individuals in organisations. They hold on to information as if it gives them power. They jealously guard and babysit information, whereas if you delegate and let other people in on the frame you get a much better quality of decision and you get more involvement: you know the whole boat rides with it.

The ability to think outside the box, lateral thinking and the ability to challenge con-structively are all vitally important. I look for people who can ask, 'Why are we doing this?', 'Are we doing this because we have always done it or because there is a good reason?' I think there are too many conformists in business at the moment.

And a fifth one is important. I call it experi-ential learning. That is the ability to adapt the theoretical to the practical via the school of hard knocks. I've been in business now about twenty-six years and I would say the first twenty were different from the last six, in the sense that when I was starting, you effectively went to third level or not, you got a job, you had your family, you might have travelled in between, you retired and you died. But you now might be starting school a wee bit later, then you go to college and do a primary degree. You then might do a master's, travel for a year or two and go back to further education. So it wouldn't be until you hit somewhere between twenty-seven and thirty that you're sitting down to your first real job. So there may be a seven-year delay before the career path even starts and I'm finding that experiential learning seems to have got lost somewhere within that process.

When I started working people went very smoothly from A to B and from C to D, learning along the way. The challenges that were there in the Ireland of the 1980s are not there now, but the difference in the challenges isn't the point. I think that too many people today have the big words for what they should be doing, but no experience.

There are people who have been out there and done things that I have never done but I don't think they have learnt a huge amount from them and I'm talking about gaining business common sense. They may have learnt a huge

amount culturally and all that kind of stuff but
are missing it in a business sense.

Denis himself is an example of someone whose career
changed drastically.

I studied industrial microbiology in UCD. I have an
interest in technical things, whether that's building
a house or building a brewery or making a beer or
pharmaceuticals or whatever but I would suggest
that my stronger passion is the communications one,
talking to people. I worked in pharmaceuticals for
a very short period and then went into Smithwicks
in Kilkenny as a trainee brewer. That was feeding
into the technical side of me. I was working in the
packaging side, which is putting stuff in bottles,
putting stuff in kegs. There was a plant closure that
came on the horizon, I was asked to look after that
as a project and that was about communicating the
issue – the problem of cost base and all that sort
of stuff – and convincing people that the decision,
which was a difficult one, was the right one. I
negotiated with these individuals on personal and
general terms, coming to an agreement with them
on hard choices. Then I went into training and
development. I moved to Dundalk and worked
as logistics manager with Guinness Ireland for a
few years. I knew nothing at all about logistics but
again these are transferable skills. For example, can
you take a concept and move it into a practical
solution? Can you communicate that solution?

Can you convince people of the correctness of that solution? So the same set of skills came into play. All those experiences were bringing me closer to human resources and ultimately to this role in Irish Distillers.

5

Outplacement and Networking

In the event of redundancy, outplacement support (using outside agencies) means different things to different companies. For bad companies, it's a sop to the staff (and unions if they're involved). It's an extra they can announce to make it look like they care. For good companies, it's proof that they really do care. When used properly, outplacement support can make a huge difference in the lives of the people forced to leave their jobs.

At its most basic, the outplacement agency should be helping you prepare your CV and getting that CV to potential employers. But it should be much more than that. It should turn a difficult and frightening time into an opportunity by identifying your strengths, offering you the chance to improve your skills, creating contacts for you, possibly generating opportunities to spend time in other companies and ultimately getting you a replacement job.

If the service you receive doesn't do that, then it's up to you. This means forgetting the job you do now and starting with a blank sheet. What do you enjoy in your job? What has made you happiest in your career to this point? What have you always wanted to do?

An important part of the process is the removal of urgency. You need to be wary of focusing on speed and pure survival. Instead, look at it in this way. You have been handed an unusual freedom. Your redundancy money will allow you to explore possibilities you might never, otherwise, have contemplated. This is, therefore, a time to play with possibilities, not focus entirely on getting a replacement post immediately.

Once you've figured what you would like to do, establish the qualifications and experience you need to do it. If the outplacer is good they'll do this with you. If they aren't, hand them your goal as a foregone conclusion. And ask for help.

It is then their task to find the courses, jobs and contacts to help you get what you want. If they're good, they will involve you at all points in the process because it is their job to prepare you to use those contacts and get those jobs. Otherwise, you are a passive product to be placed. And you're not, are you?

Most people start their job search on the internet or in newspapers, but the reality is that most people do not get jobs through the internet or newspapers.

Throughout my time helping people with their careers, I've found that somewhere in their working life there was always someone they knew who 'put them in contact with a fellow to have a chat about a job'.

In fact, this, in a convoluted way, is how I ended up heading the Career Clinic at the Communications Clinic. Two people – one a family friend, the other a cousin – got me pointed in the direction of the company where I wanted to work and one of them got me a meeting with the boss. I did the rest. I recently met a guy who owes his job to his brother-in-law. Both are happy. A female client of mine got her job through being head-hunted by a man she had worked with five years previously. When he needed someone good, he did a little research, found her and approached her. A team I'm working with in one of the banks is made up of people the boss had worked with throughout his career. You may say that's favouritism or nepotism or luck. Yeah. All of those things. Each of them has an important and crucially underestimated role to play in career-building.

'Favouritism' is the pejorative term we use to cover the boss promoting someone they like. It makes the people who don't get promoted feel better. Of course, someone shouldn't be promoted just because they 'lick up to the boss' or are a 'yes man', but the reality is that we socialise with people we like and we tend to marry people we like. So naturally, when we form a team, whether at work or play, we are more likely to create a successful team if we like the members of it. Favouritism, in that sense, is the legitimate advancement of people who are pleasant to deal with and in whom we can place trust.

Nepotism can be more problematic. Alan Crosbie, in his book about family businesses, *Don't Leave it to the Children*, issues strong warnings against the assumption that because someone is a member of a family they necessarily share some of the winning traits of the relative who founded the business. They may. They may not. Nobody should ever be given a job because of a blood relationship (although it still happens). Nobody, on the other hand, should underestimate the wider family as a network to be used to make contact with potential employers or advisers.

Luck you can't control. But you can influence it. The more positive you are in any situation, including redundancy, the more likely you are to do well in that situation.

We are now in a jobs market where the buyer is in control. And because of that, when you are made redundant, you need to muster your optimism, enlist the support of family and friends and pull out all the stops.

Above all, you need to be a good networker. Networking is keeping in contact. Some people are great at it. Those are the ones who seem effortlessly to remember birthdays; take the trouble to go to school reunions; enjoy attending events after work. The same process can be vitally important to a job-hunter because without contacts you will miss out on grapevine information about jobs that are coming on-stream, so you will be unable to use informed opportunism. Not only that, but a scarcity of contacts means that you will not have tip-of-the-tongue reference value. What you need is for a recruiter, gazing into space, suddenly to find your name on the tip of their tongue as a solution to a problem. A name doesn't find itself on the tip of anybody's tongue unless you've maintained contact with the owner of the tongue.

Look at a GAA player. Being a player or club member provides a depth and breadth of contacts and opportunities that are available to few other sportspeople. Club-level football and hurling allows for real networking that is miles away from the boozy dinners and business card swap-fests that have (unfortunately) become synonymous with the term. Good networking is not about meeting tons of people, each of them desperately hunting business. Good networking is creating and using an informal web of people with whom you actually have a relationship. You want people who can vouch for you and give you a hand. Remember that Ireland is a village, the GAA is a community and people you know are the first place to look when you're seeking an opportunity.

People like team-mates, coaches, sponsors, opponents. If you're a hurler from Wexford and want to work in the hospitality area, you call Liam Griffin (the owner of the Ferrycarrig Hotel and former Wexford hurling manager) and ask him for a steer. People like friends, ex-colleagues, relations. They love to be asked for advice and help. But the manner of asking is important. When a friend is approached in a panic, with the naked assumption that they might have a job to offer, the friend is likely to feel guilty and evasive because they simply can't help. When a friend is approached in a coolly professional way with a good CV and asked to keep at the back of their mind the possibility of recommending the CV's owner, should the opportunity arise, they are empowered to be genuinely helpful.

Like six degrees of separation, it has been suggested that any one of us in Ireland is only three contacts away from anyone we need to reach – if we really think about it. It doesn't matter whether you want to reach the Taoiseach, the President of the GAA or the editor of the *Irish Times*: the chances are that, if you work hard enough and intelligently enough, you will establish that you know someone who knows one of the three. It does help, however, if you've maintained good relationships with your contacts:

- It means keeping telephone numbers and email addresses up to date.
- It means dropping a note to someone to congratulate them when you see their promotion or wedding in the paper.
- It means making a call to people when they need consolation.

- It means having cups of coffee or the occasional lunch or dinner with old friends. Remember school and college friends. Some of today's graduates will be the leaders of industry – make sure they remember you from now on.
- It means finding ways to introduce yourself or be introduced to people you think might be interesting to know – and useful in your later career.

One client of mine – a man in his early sixties who's been phenomenally successful in different areas since he was in his twenties, adds a variation:

> You always need to be building the next network. Most people create a single career-related network. They do it in their late twenties or early thirties. By the time they're in their mid-forties, that network has lost several key links, but they may not notice. I've seen fellows creased, not just by losing their job, but by realising that the network they always assumed they could depend on doesn't really exist any more because of moves, deaths and retirements. They didn't keep building the next network.

If you network properly, it can be of enormous benefit to you in your career development. But networking is not a one-way operation. Networking operates on the same principle of all effective relationships – give and take: you must invest your time and concern in other people in order to create a context in which they are likely to invest their time and concern in you. In some quarters this is known as the favour bank, although I personally don't like the phrase, carrying, as it does, a harshly mechanical storage system for friendship.

That said, it is simply good human practice, throughout life, to be helpful to other people and to do favours for them without any immediate expectation of a quid pro quo. If you like the favour bank idea, think of it as keeping yourself in credit in the favour bank. If you don't like the favour bank idea, don't let yourself off the hook. Taking care of others is a great habit but habits are not built up by intellectual acquiescence to the concept. You have to develop some kind of reminder system to trigger you into doing what you know you should do. Regular investment in other people will make you more successful in career terms. Rather more importantly, it might also, by forcing you to think about other people in a systematic and contributory way, make you a better person.

A network is not built up overnight. But once it is built up, it means that just a phone call away are individuals who can:

- Give you information about a particular company or the context in which that company operates
- Give you a heads-up on the people who have to be reached if you're to get the job you want
- Put in a word for you
- If you don't succeed, tell you, afterwards, why you didn't get the job, so that you can do a better job on self-marketing next time round

It's important, when you set out to network, not to take the easy option. The easy option is to network only with pleasant people you like anyway. It's much more challenging – and rewarding – to network with people who on first acquaintance don't strike you as pleasant. Similarly, you must keep relationships going with people whom, at a particular point, you may want to strangle. Sometimes, this can be very difficult. It is, for example, a challenge to sustain a relationship with the manager who tells you that you're being let go. The challenge is rooted in resentment (if they're going to be kept on), frustration (if they clearly knew about it long before you did), and a deep sense of betrayal. You may know that the manager had to keep the redundancies secret, that they are mortified but grateful that their own job is currently secure and that they've explained the reason for the redundancies as well and as honestly as they were able. But you are suddenly spun loose and they're not, so the relationship changes. It is, however, important not to get pointlessly hostile to the management of the company that's now letting you go, if only because most senior managers are likely to have contacts with other senior managers. They can do a real kind of outplacement that few actual outplacement companies can do. They can sniff around, ring pals, talk to clients and get you work experience in other companies. They can get on to recruitment companies and indicate that they will be appreciative in the long term. They can ring a company like ours and say, 'Guys, I have someone here I'd like looked after.'

They will do this only: (a) if they like you; (b) if they feel sufficiently warm towards you to give you an extra leg-up; and (c) if you ask them.

Shouting at them and rejecting their help is not a good idea. Make them part of your next network – and when you have the new job, make sure you give the same kind of help to others.

Networking can help you not just in your job hunt but in showing your worth to your organisation and getting business for your company. People prefer to buy from people they like and know. They can't like and know you if they don't encounter you. In our grandparents' time, the Irish Sweepstakes, the precursor of the Lottery, had a slogan that went, 'If you're not in, you can't win.' You have to find ways physically to meet people.

Discussing networking with a client recently, I found her cynical in the extreme about the events she had attended in the name of networking over the past few years. She was particularly cynical about one executive from a very big hotel in town. He kept pitching up at these events, asking interested questions and listening. She told me:

> I couldn't imagine what he was getting out of it. It was all accountants and lawyers who were going to these events. And then, out of the blue, I had the organisation of two events landed on me at short notice. The moment I began to think about where I would locate the events, I thought of your man. When I rang him, he instantly remembered who I was and was part-way down the road before I even had to explain it. Even though he wasn't a hard-sell merchant, I still picked his hotel because I now had a business relationship with him.

She got a good deal and he got the business as a result of networking she herself saw no sense in, until the need arose.

Networking and relationship-building are key to helping your business grow and in turn developing your career. Try to make it part of your role, all day, every day. Too many organisations assume that when you make director or partner, you can then go out and start selling. The reality is that it's simply too late at that point. People can't learn how to do this stuff after twenty years working at a desk.

If you're lucky enough to be still in a job, think about a marketing diary for the next three months and a sense of the events you are going to have a presence at. You should make sure that, if a forthcoming industry event is relevant to you, you find the time, not just to be at it but to create the next network while you're there. If, for example, you're an architect and an event dealing with construction issues is going to be held in the next few months, be at it because it'll be full of quantity surveyors, architects, developers, builders and conveyancing solicitors. Just a handful of them may be worth meeting and getting to know. Don't be misled into fast-track card-swopping. It doesn't work. What must happen, in a networking situation, if it's to have long-term value to both sides, is for each to understand fully what the other does and to have developed a sense of trust in the other person. Always remember what my client noticed about the hotel executive she eventually did business with: he wasn't hard-sell, but he listened and was interested enough to ask questions. Listen. Pay attention. Don't sell. Remember that an initial meeting at an event can be the start of a relationship involving trust, work – and fun.

Some people fear networking. But try to do it early in your career. And a lot of it amounts to no more than making sure you do things that are natural. For example, if you're four or five years out of college, you'd like to maintain relationships with your college friends. Bring your postgraduate class out to lunch. For starters, it would be good simply to stay in touch. But some of your colleagues are going to be the partners of the law firms or the accountancy partnerships in ten years' time. Some of them aren't – and they're just as important. My chairman, Tom Savage, maintains that it's just as important to know the doorman as it is to know the CEO in any organisation. And he's right. Don't focus on upwardly-mobile networking. Make and maintain friendships at all levels. Something might come of it in five or ten years. It's about being visible. It's more than lunch. At the first event you're making an initial contact. After, you could go for lunch to develop the relationship. You may find out what is going on within someone else's industry and if they have any particular slant on it. Sometimes it is not networking in capital letters, it's being what the Americans call 'plugged in' to the industry. Through getting to know these individuals and building the relationships, you are getting to know whatever industry they are in.

Your network-building should start today. Write down the names of five people in business who are contacts of yours and work out a way of seeing them in the coming weeks. Start making notes and placing calls and a network will slot into place around you.

If your network doesn't cough up any contacts within a target company, all that's left to you is the salesman's dreaded cold call. This is where you contact an organisation cold, find the person in charge of hiring and try and get a meeting with them. Cold calling can be made easier by breaking it into constituent elements.

Stage one is making the research call. You should draw up your prospect list. Research the company to see who the key hirer is. Is it the CEO, managing director or the HR director, for example? You then make a phone call to verify your research with the receptionist, secretary or personal assistant. You should check the person's name (both first and second name) and confirm spelling. Don't ask to be put through to the key person on a research call – you mightn't be prepared and they might be caught on the hop. If you are asked why you want the name, explain who you are and that you wish to send a letter.

Stage two is preparing the covering letter and CV. In the letter you should introduce yourself. Give the reader a cogent reason for wanting a face-to-face meeting and be sure that it's a real benefit for them, not just for you. For example, make it clear that you understand the challenges that their company is facing and that you believe, given your experiences and skills, that you can help them to overcome those challenges. Explain that you will be making a follow-up telephone call. (By the way, a little tip with a proven record of success relates to the address on the envelope. If your handwriting is neat, handwrite it. Envelopes with handwritten addresses are more likely to be opened because they appear more personal.)

Stage three is making the follow-up call. You should ask for the contact you have researched and written to – ask for them formally. Explain to their secretary or personal assistant that you are following up on a letter. (It's your letter, but the instinctive reaction of the person answering the telephone may be that you must be responding to a letter from your contact.) Whatever you do, don't lie at any stage in the process. If asked for the more detail, give the reason for wanting a meeting – as outlined in your letter. If your contact is not available or is too busy to talk at that time, promise to call back and ask for the best time. Don't leave a voice mail. (Three or four voice mails make you seem like a stalker.) You should keep control of the process by calling back at the time you promised you'd call. Remember to be open, friendly and positive with the person who takes the call, whatever the outcome. The secretary or receptionist holds a gatekeeper post.

Stage four is confirming a meeting. When you get on to the person you believe might have the power to hire you, explain about you and why you want the meeting. Be sure to state the benefits to them of meeting you and make it clear that it would be for only fifteen minutes. It should be you who suggests a date and time for the meeting, for example, 'Would 11.15 on Friday the ninth suit?' And be sure to convey energy, enthusiasm, friendliness. It's like a sample in a supermarket. Give them a taste of your pleasant reality.

Then when you do meet them, give them hell. Remember this meeting is an interview. Be sure to prove to them that giving you fifteen minutes was the right thing to do.

6

THE COVERING LETTER AND CV – YOUR ENTRANCE TICKET

Your covering letter is generally your first interaction with a HR manager or recruiter. And often (particularly now) unless it's a damn fine covering letter, the whole package will end up in the bin. Electronic cover letters often do less than justice to the CVs they introduce because their senders think of them as afterthoughts and do not write, lay them out or proofread them with care. Cover letters on paper, together with the CVs they accompany, end up in the bin without even being read because they arrive on inappropriate paper or are crumpled, stained, cheaply self-promotional, wrongly addressed, incorrectly spelled or unprofessional in their appearance.

When writing a cover letter you should make sure first of all that the reader knows which job you're applying for. Jobs advertised in newspapers and on the Web usually include a reference code. It's there for a purpose. In fact, it's there for several purposes, including ease of administration, which is in your interest, just as much as it's in the interest of your potential employer. Don't ignore it. Include it in your letter, bold and underlined or italicised, centred above the main text. It is a courtesy that saves the recipient time and also sends a message of competence.

A cover letter should complement, not duplicate your résumé. Its purpose is to interpret the data-oriented, factual résumé and add a personal touch. This is your chance to differentiate yourself from the pack, so start with that thought. Ask yourself, 'What will the average person who applies for this job write?' The likelihood is that the average applicant will provide a bucket of generic guff about 'being a good team worker', 'seeking challenges' and 'being self-motivated'. Your task is to figure out how to write something above average. This means that you first prove you understand how the company you're writing to views themselves and reflect it back to them in your application. If they think they're the best at serving customers, write about your desire to be part of that customer service. If they believe they machine the best Woodruff keys in the world, write about your commitment to tight engineering tolerances. Basically, show that you see them as unique and special, just like they do.

Then pick one, or at most, two characteristics you have that will fit with what they need. No bull, no buzzwords; just clear specifics supported with evidence. For example: 'When I machine a Woodruff key I check it nine times with digital callipers so that it's perfect. In my last job I had the highest percentage of perfect parts among my colleagues.'

Make sure everything from spelling to the name of the recipient are accurate and handwrite the address on the envelope. Above all, if you don't understand any aspect of the job description, get it clear before you write to them (I'm sure you've already Googled 'Woodruff key').

Try to keep your covering letter to a page. Don't make the reader's life hard.

The very fact that so many people are now forced to pursue so few jobs has given rise to horrible examples, like the case of the McDonald's franchise which, while still in construction, advertised for burger flippers and was inundated with applications from lawyers, accountants and architects, all spun loose from their current place of employment, all willing to abandon prestige and high pay for any job that might help them keep up their mortgage repayments. That pressure has a negative effect on the writers of cover letters, forcing some of them into a plaintive or – even worse – raucously self-promotional tone which is inappropriate. It also causes job-seekers to write about themselves in their cover letter at appalling length. They shouldn't. You shouldn't. Put yourself in the shoes of the recipient. For every job which might, three years ago, have provoked twenty responses, they can now expect perhaps two thousand. That adds immeasurably to the task and to the tension associated with the task. A three-page begging letter at the front of your CV does nothing to help them.

Just as you keep your covering letter brief and to the point, you must try to keep your CV short. Be sure that everything on it is relevant and when in doubt, be ruthless in your editing.

Be ruthless, too, in your proofreading. Your letter and CV must be free of misprints. I was talking to a client of mine recently and I mentioned our policy of binning CVs if they contain misprints. He said that his company had done the same until 2003, when they found themselves so desperate for staff that they ignored spelling, grammar and in some cases coherence. Those days are gone. Employers are now in a position of power while simultaneously being under pressure.

They do not have the time, the patience or the necessity to tolerate messy CVs or cover letters.

Last year an Irish jobs website was attacked by hackers and CVs went to places those CVs were never meant to go. The owners of those CVs were naturally concerned about the places their personal details visited, but in fact if a CV is written properly, you should have no worries about it appearing anywhere.

Let's define our terms and specify precisely what 'written properly' means. It first of all requires you to ensure that every statement, every claim, every date and every detail in your document is factually accurate. And that you apply decent discretion.

Every now and again, people put data on CVs that should never be shared with anyone, except possibly a GP. Or the Revenue Commissioners. I see CVs containing dates of birth, marital status, numbers of kids and sexual orientation. Some even have lists of hobbies that give huge amounts of unnecessary and sometimes embarrassing details about the person. No employer needs to know if you spend your weekends travelling between Alcoholics Anonymous and Mensa (discovering you're a genius with a booze issue will be highly entertaining if your CV ends up in the hands of a third party). Under equality legislation, age, marital status and sexuality are all off-limits to potential employers. The most embarrassing mistakes on CVs are also the most common. People know they're meant to sell themselves with a CV. They also know they're likely to be sending it to a whole load of potential employers. That means we see a lot of lists of self-indulgent assertions in CVs that have no particular link to any specific job. The end result is a document that might as well be entitled 'The Wonder of Me'.

The key to a good CV is implication, not exaggeration. The objective is to provide enough detail about your experience for the prospective employer to deduce your skills from your experience. All you have to do is imply. All they have to do is infer. Wild, unsupported boasts are not the way to go, yet when job applicants bring me their CVs for editing, I regularly find them littered with statements like, 'I am a great communicator; I am a people person; I am hungry and enthusiastic.' These statements read like the empty self-promotion that they are. Not only are they assertions without evidence – a lethal form of unmemorable, unpersuasive communication – but they're yellow-pack assertions which every second job applicant makes. It's much better to illustrate quickly the communications requirements of your last job, indicate how you met those requirements and let the employer work out himself or herself that you're a good communicator. If Tiger Woods wants to prove he's a gifted golfer, he doesn't write, 'I am an excellent golfer.' He writes that he won more Masters titles – faster – than anyone in history. Inference does the rest.

A number of simple steps are involved in writing the perfect CV:

1. Start with your most recent employment experience.
2. Through that experience, show how you demonstrated the skills required for the job for which you're now applying.
3. Don't make sweeping assertions about your talents.
4. Give the evidence and let the employer judge.
5. (And this is the most important consideration of all)

> Tailor the CV (and the covering letter) to the specific job.

A generic CV is hugely disrespectful to the receiver; it's like whipping out an engagement ring and telling your girlfriend, 'I've fired this at a few girls over the years, how about you wear it? Ah go on, I'm an excellent communicator…'

If your CV is evidence-based, clear and focused on the employer it will increase your chances of netting the job.

In the current employment climate, CVs simply have to contain elements that get the HR person saying, 'I wouldn't mind talking to this man/woman.' The requisite experience will have to be specified and expanded upon to show not just what you did but what you gained from it. Every piece of experience you cite should prove a skill, not an occurrence.

This last element is crucially important and worth a little more attention. A key deficit in most CVs is that a job applicant lists experiences they have had, without establishing, for their prospective employer, precisely how the experiences matter. I regularly see CVs which list promotions and project work as skeletally as if the writer were putting together the details of a train timetable. This happens because the writer feels the experience speaks for itself. It doesn't. You were part of a project introducing a new product into the plant. You state that. You assume that the prospective employer will say to themselves something along the following lines:

> Oh, my goodness, this is exactly the person we need. She can work in a team. She can handle a product with which she's had no previous experience. She can bring a project in on time and within budget, so

it's fair to assume that she pays attention to detail
and keeps an eye on what money is being spent...

Why should employers do this for you? Why should
they go to all the trouble of explaining to themselves the
implications you should explain to them? Bluntly, they won't.
Besides, even if they were willing to do your job for you, they
might not be able to work out the significance of events that
seems obvious to you.

I'm not suggesting your CV should turn into a seventeen-
page epic description of the wonders of you. Just that you
shouldn't just use it to establish what happened to you. It
should demonstrate what you've learned from what happened
to you, or what skills you demonstrated – and how both would
be useful to you in the job you're now applying for.

That said, do not put everything that ever happened to
you in your CV. Lots of people become parents, for instance,
but to claim that on a CV as if it provided some kind of
benefit to the potential employer would be weird. Now, the
parent may know that becoming a mother or father taught
them restraint, helped them to budget for the first time or
made them learn songs they can sing around the water cooler
in three-part harmony. But the value of these things is not
immediately apparent to the potential employer. They just
look at the claim and think, 'Why the hell would anybody
put "parenthood" on their CV?'

Now, OK, I know you would never put something as silly
as that in your CV. But when you have drafted the document,
make sure an equivalent howler hasn't snuck in. For example,
the fact that you buzzed off to Australia to find yourself and
that it took you two years may be of great importance to you,

but has no relevance to a potential employer. If you want to mention it, make sure to include illustrations of how the Oz experience developed skills or understanding in you that will be useful in the job for which you're applying. Or that the experience allowed you to deploy a pre-existing skill or talent.

Once you have drafted your CV, go back through it to make sure that if you state, for example, that you managed a group of people, the evidence is included to prove you did it well. Interrogate every experience:

- If you negotiated a deal, what shows you got a good outcome?
- If you planned a strategy, what proves it was any good?

A vital aspect of a good CV is that it differentiates you from all other applicants. The reason for this is that other (well prepared) candidates are likely to have similar educational qualifications and experience. If they have cop-on, they will present themselves, in print, with clarity and professionalism. The result is that two good CVs – two reasonably similar CVs – may land on the recruiter's desk. In that situation, you want your CV to stand out and to contain points which differentiate you from the other candidate. Which means that, wherever possible, you insert differentiators. Anything that makes you different. Better. More interesting than the other contenders.

Sport is arguably the most useful differentiator. For example, the simple presence of a sporting pedigree can get you noticed; a Minor All-Ireland, a county championship, a club medal, climbing Everest – these are all factors that separate you from the field. More importantly, they're all things that say, 'I can excel in my chosen field.'

A CV must include the following:

- Name and personal details
- Personal Profile
- Educational achievements and qualifications
- Employment history
- Relevant interests and achievements/hobbies and pastimes
- Referees

The personal profile gives a quick overview at the start. You should keep the information concise and relevant. It should include your strengths and qualities, your business skills and your career goals. (And don't make a big issue of your goals. A prospective employer doesn't need to know that you want to travel the world, work for Bill Gates in Africa and head up a multinational in Beijing. Keep your goal short-term, singular and related directly to what this specific company wants of you. Try to cast it in terms that serve them, rather than you. Don't say, 'I want an interesting job meeting people,' if you can say, 'Because I'm good at quickly creating good relationships with strangers, I would be able to join and contribute to the sales force at the Joe Bloggs company without delay.')

People put the strangest things under the hobbies and pastimes heading, on the assumption that it makes them seem like rounded individuals. Or because they believe a wide range of interests is expected to be listed. It isn't. Keep that bit simple and short. Too many outside interests make it look like you spend your entire life playing football and hurling, visiting the cinema and theatre, reading Tolstoy, working out, gardening, fire-eating, performing amateur dramatics, feeding the homeless and on and on. Some are just bizarre things you shouldn't put there at all. Socialising, for example, is neither a hobby nor an interest. It's drinking dressed up as a pastime. The litmus test is whether or not whatever you put in under this heading feeds into the skillset for the job you are after. For example if you are going for a position as a PR account executive, a genuine interest in current affairs is a must and your having worked as an unpaid PR officer for a sporting group, charity or aspiring politician indicates that you're already coming to terms with some of the realities of the job for which you've applied.

The current wrong-headed fashion is to put a photograph on your CV. Why is this wrong-headed? Because a CV is designed to illustrate your ability to do the job and give a sense of what you can offer. Unless you are applying for a job as a model, actor or *Blue Peter* presenter, a picture makes no positive contribution. A picture will never influence an employer to hire you but it could influence them not to. Employers can't legally discriminate against you because of age, colour, gender or appearance but there's no reason to test this. The risk that they might not like the look of you is a pointless one that you do not need to run.

The key to a good CV is to provide enough detail about your experience to make it unavoidably obvious to the prospective employer that you have the required skills. While it might be tempting to include a photo so that the employer thinks you're beautiful or have a great haircut, it's a temptation to be resisted. Competent employers will have a set of criteria. They'll make a decision based on your track record and expertise, not your looks.

Picking your referees is important. Your primary school teacher may think you were the cutest kid in her First Communion class but a prospective employer will gain nothing from her historic validation of your general cuteness. He or she wants evidence of your current competence from two people who can attest to it with some credibility. That can mean a lecturer in the university at which you studied, your former employer, a senior colleague where you worked, or even the boss of a charity where you did volunteer work.

It's obviously awkward to ask your current employer for a reference if they don't know of your plan to seek employment elsewhere, whereas most employers, if they're cutting back and would welcome a reduction in head count, would be delighted to give you a super reference.

On the other hand, at least one of the companies that uses the Communications Clinic for recruitment advice has a 'no reference' policy. It's not personal. They've just found it simpler, when asked for a reference, to send a note confirming that the employee worked in their company from such-and-such a year until the present and had the title or role of X. If you have any reservations about naming people as referees, state the reservation on your CV: you can supply referees if required, but it would clearly be inappropriate to seek a reference from your current employer at this time.

Check with your prospective referees before you put their names, titles and phone numbers in your CV. And, if they're happy for you to do so, go one step further. Prompt them with what you'd like them to say:

Listen, because this job is all about high level discretion, is there any chance, when they ring you, that you could tell them I never gossiped and was punctilious in taking care of my notebook computer and flash drives, so you were always sure no confidential information would get out into the public?

Remind your referee of events and achievements in your career which they may have forgotten, so that they're at the top of their mind when the new employer telephones them.

The final hugely important step to take, when you're satisfied that your CV meets all the criteria, is to proofread it.

You'd be surprised how many people do not do this. Or, if they do it, do it badly.

Here's how to proof your CV. Print out two hard copies. Give one of them to a friend, your mother, your partner or a colleague. Tell them you want them to go into a room on their own, without their mobile phone, and hunt for misprints. Tell them your entire future may hinge on them catching an error before you send the thing out.

Then take the other copy and go into a room on your own without your mobile phone. Start at the end, not at the beginning. The reason for this is that, as we read something in the sequence with which we are familiar, we make an unconscious assumption that it is correct. In other words, we see what we expect to see, even if it's not there. The benefit to starting at the end is that it interrupts this cognitive loop and forces your brain cells to take in the text as if it were new to them.

Starting at the end, read each and every sentence out loud. It's when you read something out loud that you spot mistakes. Put an asterisk, not just beside any mistake you spot, but beside any name, date or detail that you assume to be correct. When you've finished your reverse-read, check each one of those names, dates and details one more time. Then retrieve the second copy from the other reader. Match the two of them up against each other and – once you've taken care of anything either of you has identified as a problem – you're good to go.

Well, nearly good to go. Before you send it off, make sure you have the correct name, title and address on the envelope or on the email. It's deeply irritating, if your name is Margot Kinnear and if you're the Head of HR in Joe Bloggs's company, to have to open a letter addressed to Margo Kinner, Head of HR in Jo Bloggs company. More to the point, it may make Margot decide, long before she reads your cover letter or opens your CV, that your attention to detail and respect for the people with whom you want to work is not exactly award-winning. So a little, final, obsessive checking does no harm.

Once you've got the CV in the door, the next task is to prepare for the interview.

INDUSTRY VIEW: KARL MANNING, DIRECTOR OF RETAIL SALES, HALIFAX

> Starting at the start, I always look to ensure a CV is well laid out, contains no spelling mistakes and no contradictions. Contradictions could imply that the candidate is being slightly economical with the truth so it begs the question: what else are they

prepared to be economical with? Particularly in a bank, honesty is a must-have trait. A pet hate is the use of acronyms without an explanation. It's very hard for the assessor to make a call on an application if it's not understood. I would expect 'CRM (Customer Relationship Management)', for example. I'm personally always interested in hobbies. To me, sports say they have experience in working as part of a team, which is always a positive in banking and in most professions.

The Elements of a CV

PERSONAL PROFILE

A profile gives a quick overview at the start. It is the first thing that the reader will see, so make sure that it's concise and relevant. A profile can include a description of yourself; your qualities and strengths; your track record and business skills; your career goals; and a summary of your main skills relevant to the job in question.

SUMMARY OF EDUCATION AND QUALIFICATIONS

- Dates
- University/college attended
- Degree
- Grades
- Major Subjects

Start with the most recent qualifications. Include any subjects studied that may be relevant to the job.

PROFESSIONAL EXPERIENCE

Date: from-to
Name of company
- Key job role
- Brief description of what you did
- Skills developed in this role
- Achievements
- Successes and scale of success

Start with the most recent job and work backwards. Give most space to most recent and relevant jobs. Include all relevant jobs and emphasise skills gained in each job.

INTEREST/ACHIEVEMENTS (OR SEPARATE HEADINGS)

Interests

- Include a broad range
- Include individual and group interests

Achievements

- Use bullet points and be concise
- Give range of academic and personal achievements

JOHN LENNON

Address
Phone
Email

PERSONAL PROFILE

I am a proactive and enthusiastic graduate in Economics and Politics with the ability to work as part of a team or independently. I have the ability to communicate effectively with customers and colleagues alike. I have developed an excellent eye for detail and the ability to meet deadlines.

EDUCATION AND QUALIFICATIONS

2007 to present
DIT Aungier Street, Dublin 2
      Postgraduate Diploma in Legal Studies (Exams this May)
2004-2007
University College Dublin, Belfield, Dublin 4
      BA Economics and Politics: 1st Class Honours
1999-2004
Ardscoil Rís, Griffith Avenue, Dublin 9
      Leaving Certificate in English, Maths, Business, Economics, History, Gaeilge and Physics. Total points: 510 out of a possible 600.

PROFESSIONAL EXPERIENCE

2006 to present
ABC Insurance
- Sales and Customer Service Agent
- Delivered excellent customer service and advice to customers on the phone and face to face
- Consistently exceeded monthly sales and service targets by at least 10%
- Developed organisational and administrative skills
- Awarded customer service agent of the month for quality service

INTEREST/ACHIEVEMENTS

- First Class Honours in Economics and Politics
- Captain of Fingallians GAA club
- Raised €25,000 for Médecins Sans Frontières

REFEREES

Available upon request

7

The Job Interview – Your Time to Dazzle

If you get your interviewing skills right, you can sell yourself to a particular interviewer. If you don't, then all the time, creativity, money and research in the world won't get you the job you want.

One of the first big problems to overcome when preparing for a job interview is that of attitude. Too often, interviewees or job applicants see themselves in a subservient role. They're the ones 'begging for the job'. So they concede the dominant role to the interviewee, who, as they see it, holds all the aces, making it a very uneven encounter. Their view of their own subservience feeds into their behaviour, so they act as if they're at an oral exam for which they know they've done insufficient homework. They are destroyed before they ever get to present the reasons they should get the job. Destroyed by an incorrect understanding of the interview process.

The fascinating thing is that, from the interviewer's point of view, the encounter is just as difficult. The way they see it, they're the one under pressure, the one who has to fill the vacancy, the one who's going to be judged on whether they got the right candidate or picked a shocker.

An interviewer working for a small company is under

particular pressure, knowing that a wrong decision could cripple the business. A recent piece of research showed that a wrong hire could cost the company three times the salary of the person. So it can be a costly thing to get wrong. An interviewer working for a very large company is under double pressure. First of all, an initial screening may have been done by a recruitment company (although this is happening less and less as companies are finding it hard to justify the extra cost). So if the interviewer manages to find a shocker among the select few proffered by the head-hunter and reject them as part of the interview process that's a kind of negative achievement. The recruiter has saved the company from a disaster. However, the very fact that the head-hunting company has suggested that a potential recruit is worth interviewing may mislead the interviewer into rating them more highly than they should be rated.

The bad news for a recruiter is that if this happens and the inadequate candidate is selected and working as a member of staff, it doesn't matter what the head-hunting agency recommended. As far as the company is concerned, their own interviewer is the one responsible for the selection car crash and their line manager will let the interviewer know, in no uncertain terms, that as a recruiter, he's a gobshite. That's become even more likely – and more dangerous – because of the economic downturn. During the Celtic Tiger, mistakes in recruitment could be forgiven; now they won't be.

A job interview is, therefore, a much more evenly balanced encounter than most job applicants appreciate. A job interview is, in fact, a very simple interaction. One side of the table has a problem – they need to have a position filled. The other side of the table may be the solution to that problem. And it's down to the interviewee to prove that they are that solution. Interviewees should approach the interview as a problem-solving exercise in which they are putting themselves forward as understanding the needs represented by the vacancy and as the best solution to those needs.

Accordingly, every job interview should be approached, from the applicant's point of view, with this attitude: 'I understand what your company is doing, I know what you're trying to achieve with this appointment and I believe that what I can offer you will help you to achieve that.'

Obvious? Of course it is. Except that many job applicants, especially in bad economic times, go into an interview with quite a different attitude, such as: 'Gimme the job because I need it.'

The freedom to be able to adopt the correct attitude to the interview will come about only through a thorough understanding of what you have to offer and how that can be related to the needs of the target company. The key to success here is through proper preparation with this goal: *At the end of the interview, the experiences and capabilities of the interviewee will be known, understood and clearly related to the position on offer.*

That's it. That's all you can achieve. But if you achieve it, you've radically improved your chances of appointment.

There are no secret techniques or tricks to make you better than you actually are. People who spoof or hype or generally indulge in overselling are on a loser from the moment they open their mouths. A successful job applicant tells it straight; is understandable, credible and memorable. They communicate to the interviewer the reality of what they are and present the best of that reality. They don't spout learned-off answers from books, or produce monosyllabic responses that make them seem dull and bored, not to mention boring.

In order to do an honest, authentic and impressive interview, you have to start, not with yourself, but with the person people on the other side of the table and with the company they represent. That's true of all communication: you need to understand the people that you are communicating with. If you want to persuade your mother to mind your toddler for a couple of days, you start by working out how your mother thinks, what else she might be doing and how best – knowing her – you can convince her that child-minding would be a great addition to her coming week. Yet, oddly, when we set out to make presentations, we retreat from the people we need to influence and concentrate instead on ourselves. In just the same way, when we go for job interviews, we tend to start with our wonderful (or perhaps our terrified) selves, rather than beginning with the people we want to go and work for.

Well in advance of the interview itself, you can set yourself up for a win by doing two kinds of research. One aspect of research will give you a good sense of the kind of company to which you're applying. Their history. Their track record. Their brand. Their reputation. Their products and services. Their culture.

This matters. Now, let's be honest: it may not, right now, matter to you. You may be so desperate to get gainful employment that you'd happily sign on with Vlad the Impaler Plc and not be that bothered by the details of impaling. But it sure as hell matters to Vlad. Each company regards themselves as unique – even if they're in the same kind of business as other companies – and they want job applicants to yearn to work, specifically, with them, not just see them as one of a line of possible and equally acceptable employers. So learn the company before you pitch up in front of an interviewer as a possible future employee.

The second kind of research, in one sense, is simpler. It's working out precisely what is required by the job. In many cases, the advertisement will carry the necessary details, but in some cases, it will also carry an indicator that further information is a) available on their website or b) can be forwarded to you on request. The extra information you need is a complete job specification. When you have the advertisement and the job specification in front of you, isolate each and every requirement listed. Each one of them represents a keyhole into which you must insert a key.

This preparatory work is an essential – if tedious – part of your job interview preparation, because, long before you sit down in front of them, you must be clear about precisely what the interview panel need in the person they select. You must understand the key skills or competences required for this position. Once you know what the employer is looking for and have broken down the list of skills you need to do the job, then you have some hope of preparing for an interview, so that you can prove you can do it under pressure in a short space of time.

People think that we in the Communications Clinic put words in people's mouth and paint a veneer on job-seekers so that they sell a phoney version of themselves. In fact, my Chairman, Tom Savage describes what we're in as the transport business. What he means by this is that lots of people are good communicators when they're talking to people they know and like. They just can't transport that good communicator into pressurised situations. We help them transport their own reality. We never offer them answers or formulae of words. That would be dishonest. We work with the person until they can transport their authentic self into the worrying context of a job interview. That way, what they produce will be the truth, the impression they leave with the recruiter will be authentic and, if they are appointed, they will be in a position to take up the post with some confidence that they'll genuinely be able to do the job.

A number of skills are common to all roles: technical qualifications, communication skills and customer focus show up on 75 per cent of job descriptions. Job descriptions are a good guide, but if you don't have one to hand – if it's one of those posts where the advertisement is considered to be all the information applicants need – sit down and work out what skills you need to do the job well. For example, if you're going for a job as a bank manager, in addition to a commerce degree and experience in the financial services industry, you will be required to demonstrate specific relevant skills. You're going to need management skills, business acumen and an ability to meet deadlines.

Similarly, if you're going for a job as an engineer, while you will require relevant third-level qualifications, you will also, typically, need team-working skills, problem-solving skills, crisis management, an attention to detail and an understanding of the industry. The easiest way to figure out what's required is to ask yourself what your first day at work would be like and what skills you would deploy. If it's a day of meetings, you need communications skills. If you're starting with a team briefing, you need to be able to motivate staff. If you're going to be digging through the sales figures for a division, you need numeracy and a capacity to analyse.

Once you have figured out the individual skills and competences required by the successful applicant for this particular job, isolate each one and get to work on it.

You can't just claim to be good at, say, numeracy and sales figures analysis. On the day of the interview, you must be able to prove each claim you make. Not only must you prove it, you must be able to make it interesting to the people listening to you: they must get illustrations of your ability through examples of past experience. If you say in the interview, 'I can manage people,' the response will be some form of 'Prove it.' If you're lucky. If you're not lucky and if the interviewers, having gone through this same process with ten people over the previous day and a half, have lost the will to live, they will also have lost the will to interrogate you in your own best interest and may simply leave your assertion hanging in the air, unchallenged, unevidenced. To be effective, you need to have more than a list of one-line assertions and claims to the competences that would allow you to do the job. Remember, the interview isn't an oral examination. You need to be active with your information and offer lots of examples. It isn't the job of the panel to drag the information out of you. Indeed, I would hold that they shouldn't bother, because the lack of preparation and hunger demonstrated by your passivity is, in itself, a disqualifier. It suggests that, under even mild pressure, you go into your shell and don't bother to solve the other person's problems. Why should they employ a leaden self-absorbed lump like the one you seem to be?

When preparing your answers and examples you should try to operate within a four-layer structure.

The first layer is the general. Your instinct may be to begin by answering a question on budgets by stating something like this: 'Yes, I have experience in managing budgets and I've been successful many times.'

In the interview phase of a competition, you can be pretty sure everyone in their right mind being interviewed will say that. But if they leave their answer at that first level, they should be shot, because they have failed to differentiate themselves from the other applicants who will make the same claim in – probably – almost the same words. Moving on to the second level is vital.

The second level is the specific. Differentiation begins when you become specific. This second level is what initiates your separation from the rest of the contenders. In your preparation sit down and figure out your most impressive example for each skill. Keep one in reserve as backup. The specific is where you give details like when and where it happened, what you did, how you did it, how you handled particular challenges, what resources you employed to meet them, what initiatives you took, which decisions you implemented and why. Don't forget to tell the interviewer what happened at the end of the process: what was the outcome. And be sure that it's a success. All these details will be particular to you and will give you the opportunity to stand out from others. You must seek to give detailed, interesting, anecdotal but not self-indulgent examples of your experiences, so that no doubt is left in your interviewer's mind as to what you are capable of doing.

Level three is the key learning or insight gained. This refines the differentiation. It's at this level that you communicate what it was that you got from each of the individual experiences. Very few people do this. They think that just because they've said they've done something, the interviewer will figure out how they've developed as a result and how it enhances their capabilities for the future. To expect an interviewer to do this is taking a very big chance on the single most important issue of the whole interview: the accurate translation of past experiences into present and future capabilities.

It isn't the interviewer's job to interpret you in the best possible light. It's your job to make that kind of interpretation inevitable and inescapable. Just do it: analyse each of your experiences, positive and negative, and tell how they've affected your development and understanding. Two great advantages come from doing this. Firstly, those personal insights are unique. They set you apart. Secondly, they make the interviewer's job infinitely easier by doing the translation process from experience to potential for him or her. The right question may never come, so don't wait for it. And don't assume the interviewer can – or should – read your mind.

Level four is relating your experience to the job on offer. This is where you relate each individual experience directly to the job for which you have applied, thus completing the cycle of understanding for the interviewer and leaving nothing to chance, nothing to be figured out and no opportunity for ambiguity. When candidates fail to relate their example to the role, it can create a 'that was then' mindset in the interviewer.

Properly managed, the process takes the interviewer through each experience like this:

1. General: Yes, I have experience in skill A. And I have been successful many times in using it.
2. Specific: Here, specifically, is what I did in one situation requiring that skill, how I did it and why I went about it this way. Here are some of the challenges

I overcame during it. Here's how it was rated in terms of the end result.

3. Key learning/insight gained: Here's how I have developed as a result: the insights gained, the skills refined, the judgement acquired.

4. Relate it: And here's how I can apply that learning to this role.

PREPARATION

Earlier I wrote that it's crucial to take the initiative in an interview and move it away from an examination. If you illustrate your skills and abilities properly, they should be evocative and memorable to your interviewer. At the end of a day's interviewing when the panel are asking themselves, 'Who was good at management?', you want them saying, 'Pat was. His example of managing and motivating that team in Halifax was superb.'

I cannot overstate the importance of examples and anecdotes in the job interview or, indeed, in any communication. Every culture, race or religion uses stories, examples and anecdotes in their communication. If you look at the parables, for example, you will realise that, despite having been created over two thousand years ago, they are still referenced today. The people who came up with the parables had important concepts to communicate to different audiences. But they did not outline the concept. Instead, what they did was to use anecdotes each audience could identify with, so that they could make the concept interesting, understandable and memorable. They did it well. They created good stories with a moral punch. The end result is that, to this day, people will describe someone as a 'good Samaritan' or a 'prodigal son'.

In any job interview, you are required to put a concept into the heads of the interviewers. That concept is the idea that you can do the job and do it better than anyone else. However, simply stating that concept in conceptual language won't work. The only way you can make it stick is by illustrating your claimed ability by using past examples. Because those examples are true, actually happened and are unique to you, they'll be interesting. Because you're showing the interviewer what you did in the past, you're creating the understanding that you can do it again in the future. If you cast your experience in the form of a story – because anecdote is a memorable communication structure – and present them with concrete examples, making sure those examples are relevant to them, they'll remember them. And they'll remember you.

Good examples must spring to mind when you are under pressure and they will not do this unless you work on them in advance. Outline each example in as few words as possible on individual cards. Now, shuffle the cards. Pick the first one to offer itself. Expand on that skill and give examples by going through the levels, seeking to make it desperately interesting. Shuffle again and talk about the next one that offers itself. Do this often enough and you will become comfortably familiar with the content of each block and its logical flow.

You cannot prepare for every question but you can prepare yourself to have the mindset that your job is to meet the employer's needs. More to the point, if you prepare a series of interesting and relevant inputs, any incoming question will allow you to select from within a wealth of good material, rather than creating a 'How do I answer this?' confusion in your mind. It's important to stress that preparing in the way I have outlined radically changes the entire interview. Instead of an interrogation which you're secretly convinced is setting out to identify your weaknesses, the interview becomes an opportunity for you to enumerate your strengths and expand on them.

Now, before we look at the questions you're likely to get, let's go back to the priority I mentioned earlier. You must start with the people who are interviewing you. It helps if you know who they are. Quite often, if you check with the company or organisation in advance, they'll be happy to tell you who's on the interview panel. You can Google them and learn about them – perhaps even get a sense of what they look like. All this broadens your comfort zone.

Even if they don't tell you in advance, they're likely to tell you on the day. The receptionist may have a list of the participants on the panel and you lose nothing by asking. If nobody tells you in advance, they will tell you when you go in. That's the moment when you must turn down the volume of the static in your head and concentrate fiercely on getting the names right. If you don't catch one, ask for it again. Use it in your greeting: 'Dr Buggins, how do you do?'

Normally, the person in charge of an interview panel, or the interviewer, if it's one of those encounters requiring only one person to put the questions, will set out to put you at your ease at the beginning. This is your chance to listen to their outlining of the process and to indicate, by your attitude, that you're glad to be there. Just as it's their job to make you comfortable and at your ease, it's your job to establish a warm, willing and pleasant response to their welcome. Remember, if you smile at them, the very act of smiling reduces your own blood pressure and sends a message to your brain that you're not under attack. Do not be in a mad rush to get to the meat of the encounter – the first impression you give by being affable and confident is important too.

The opening question in any interview tends to be a soft and open one. 'Open' in the sense that it allows the interviewee lay out what they would like to put on the table. And the great thing is that once it's out on the table, it increases the likelihood that the interviewer will follow the lead you have established. An opening question could be, 'Talk me through your CV', or, 'Tell us a little bit about yourself.'

This is not an invitation for you to provide a guided tour through your gravestone details. It is an opportunity to explain the significance and relevance of each of the stages of your career or educational path. Your CV isn't enough to get you the job. It's enough to get you the interview. It's the interview that will get you the job. During the interview, regard the CV as the brochure that hooked them enough to get you to this point but don't make any of these mistakes that I've seen in my Career Clinic interviews:

- Suggesting to the interviewer that they should refer to a particular page in the CV. They're not your students, obediently following a lecturer's instructions to locate a page in a textbook and are likely to be uncomfortable if you so direct them.
- Selling the CV, not yourself. Constant references to a CV are pointless. The employer is not offering your CV a job. It's you they want or don't want.
- Failing to expand on something that's featured in the CV because it's dealt with in the CV.

It's your responsibility to make the experiences briefly outlined on paper become real to the interviewer.

Whether it's the interviewer's first question or the last question, it should be listened to in a concentrated respectful way. Don't be so eager to answer that you don't wait for the end of the question. Even if the intent of the questioner is obvious to you and even if you have a devastatingly good answer, stay silent until the questioner is done. To you, a question may be simple and obvious. The person putting the question to you doesn't need to know that's how you see it. Pausing to consider a question is flattering to the questioner, so don't behave as if the question was bog standard, obvious and beneath your great mind – and above all don't deliver the insulting comment: 'I get asked that a lot.'

The reality, of course, is that some of the questions will not be welcome to you. But even the most negative question should not come as a surprise to you. If you prepare properly, every logical question, no matter how much of a stinker it is, should be foreseen.

You must never lie in an interview. It's your responsibility, in advance of any interview, to work out what, in your track record, might be viewed with suspicion by the interviewer. Watch out for gaps in your CV. One of those gaps can be the result of your having been made redundant. Elsewhere in this book, I deal with the issues facing executives who have suffered job cuts as a result of the recession. The point I'm making here is that if you are among the thousands of people who have been 'let go', you must not make a negative decision about yourself based on that experience. You didn't cause the recession. You've been thumped by the recession, true, but it hasn't robbed you of your qualifications, experience and competence. However, let's be realistic. Few experiences are as personally devastating as having your employment terminated unexpectedly.

In previous recessions, cutbacks, downsizing and redundancies tended to be worse for the unskilled or less skilled. It's different, this time around. The jobs of architects, surveyors and real estate salespeople are being terminated by their employers. Nor is the carnage confined to areas obviously related to construction. Solicitors and other professionals are also finding themselves jobless.

When it happens, it's more than a personal blow. It's a demolition of expectations and norms that can be devastating for individuals. No matter how clear it is that the entire economy has tanked and that redundancy is a consequence of a wider disaster, not the result of personal performance failure, many of the highly-qualified jobless find their confidence grievously diminished by the experience. It's the first time in history that the implicit promise on which so many careers are built has been broken. That implicit promise was: work hard, get a good degree and put in a good performance on the job. Most of us spend most of our time at work. Our social connectedness starts there. So when the rules of life, as applied to the workplace, change so radically and with so little warning, the shock to the individual is enormous. Every day, in my Career Clinic, I meet bright competent achievers who are frankly ashamed about what has happened to them.

This unearned shame greatly complicates their job-seeking. Every time they identify an appealing post calling for all the qualifications and experience they have, they agonise about one question they know they will be asked in the interview: 'Why did you leave the job you were in?' They cannot figure out a way to tell a prospective employer that they have been made redundant and are convinced that having been let go indicates they were inessential in the previous post, and that on these grounds the prospective employer will immediately decide against them if they tell the truth.

Not so. Telling the truth as early as possible in a recruitment interview is not only the honourable way to deal with the issue but the route to employment. The key step, before the question surfaces, is to put yourself in the position of the prospective employer. What's the advantage to them in your candidacy? In many cases, the person who has been made redundant has valuable experience and a proven track record. They wouldn't have been presenting those advantages to a prospective employer had the economy continued to bowl along as it did in the previous decade. So the prospective employer gains rather than loses by selecting someone recently let go.

Just make sure you have done enough research on the company to which you've applied. Research will allow you to match the skills you gained and deployed in your previous job to the requirements of the new employer. Candidates also need to have rehearsed, out loud, the story of what happened to their previous employer. The story must be clear, truthful and discreet. In its telling, the candidate must, in effect, say, 'This is the kind of person I am. Loyal to the employer I was with. Understanding of the legal necessity to remove the most recently-hired, even if the employer wanted to keep some of them – like me. And buoyant in the face of a temporary set-back, which had nothing to do with how well I was doing in the job.'

Talking to your previous employer about the reference they will give, in writing or verbally, is pivotal. The shame experienced by the person who is made redundant is matched, in most cases, by the misery of their boss. No employer is comfortable with downsizing and most are eager to assuage the guilt – for themselves and the employee – by vouching for the employee's capacities when asked.

By the way, one of the reasons you bought this book is that, although you're still in a job, you figure that you might lose that job in the foreseeable future, so let's look, here, at worst-scenario planning. Redundancies rarely come without warning. It is therefore imperative that, if you believe you may find yourself without a job in the next six months, you get on to the jobs market now, rather than later. But even if you are made redundant, you have to do more than job-seek in the months thereafter. Regard yourself as responding to one imperative: the prevention of a gap in your CV. Try to get a lecturing position, go back to college, get some personal development training, do volunteer work or present yourself to a company for free to gain work experience in some area of your CV which could usefully be beefed up.

Another question that will crop up is, 'What was it about this job and company that caught your eye?' Each company (like every person) has a sense of individuality. Accountancy giant KPMG, for example, sees itself as being quite different to Deloitte. Irish Distillers may be in the same business sector as Diageo, but it regards itself as having a very different history and corporate culture. The first moments of an interview should establish your understanding of the company and the job. They should not let the HR manager know that you basically want any job at this level in any company. They will quickly lose interest in you if you have demonstrated no interest in them.

In the private sector, the style of interviewing varies, although, increasingly, companies seek training for their interviewers to ensure they stay within the law and can move the interview beyond good or bad impressions into something more substantive and evidence-based. Competency-based interviewing is a method that is being used more regularly now to identify the best candidate for the job, particularly in the civil and public service. If you are going for promotion in either of those sectors, you will know in advance the competences you must prove. The best structure for your answers, as given earlier in this chapter, still applies. Competency-based interviewing is much more regulated and less exciting. It obviates the possibility that you'll be asked wide-blue-yonder questions like, 'What would you do to resolve the Middle-East conflict?'; 'What did you think of the story on the front page of today's *Irish Times* about the social partners?'; or, 'How would you handle your department if an earthquake drove Ireland and Britain together?'

All these questions were actually asked of candidates before competency-based interviews became the norm. Back then, some interviewers thought they were pop-psychologists and believed they'd just 'know the right person when they met them'. Interviews, back then, tended to have the same pace and recklessness of a bob-sled ride and gave the interviewee no control at all. They were more exciting but a lot less productive.

Competency-based interviews have become the standard process for financial institutions, companies and government departments because they avoid the random and unfair. They focus interviewers and interviewees on specifics and evidence. They create a consistency across all the interviews. Everyone is asked the same questions. In addition, the interviewers prepare the criteria on which they are going to grade the answers and the weighting to be applied to different areas. It is expected, in this context, that the interviewee will prepare specific answers for the questions. The competency-based interview is viewed as fair. It is certainly an easy interview format to prepare for, as it is specifically designed to allow the interviewee to illustrate their ability through past experiences.

In addition to the experience questions, interviewers may ask what are called 'scenario questions'. This is where an interviewer outlines a particular scenario and asks what the job applicant would do in that situation. Scenario questions are valuable on a number of fronts. They're valuable to the interviewer, because they give the opportunity to observe how the candidate listens, how they analyse and how they approach problem-solving.

In addition, they move a candidate out of commentator mode. Some candidates are extremely impressive when they're commenting on issues like diversity or conflict as theoretical propositions, but may be markedly less impressive when presented with a hypothetical situation and asked precisely how they would respond in these circumstances.

When asked a scenario question, the first thing you must do is demonstrate that you have listened and understood what is being asked. If necessary, feed back what you have heard and ask if you've left anything out. The next thing you must do is think. It sounds obvious, but many interviewees are convinced that if they don't fill the air with words during every moment of a job interview, in some way they are failing.

An interviewer or interview panel wants to assess what you would be like if you were appointed to the job. If it's a senior appointment requiring judgement, the scenario question provides you with the opportunity to demonstrate judgement by considering all the implications of the problem presented to you. It's very useful to refer to an experience akin to the scenario, which illustrates your competence. (See: we're back to those past experiences.)

Interviewers may also ask you negative questions:

- What are your weaknesses?
- What's the worst mistake you've made?
- What's been your biggest setback?

Inexperienced interviewees become extremely anxious when asked negatively-phrased questions. But a negative question gives a golden opportunity for a positive answer. Just make sure it isn't an obviously prepared answer. The question everyone hates is, 'What's you greatest weakness?' The answer everyone hates is, 'Well, I suppose I'm a bit of a perfectionist.' This answer reeks of bad advance preparation, since it clearly is not a weakness but a strength presented as one.

Other horrific responses to the weakness question are, 'I take on too much work,' or, 'I hate letting things go.' Quite apart from being crudely self-serving, these responses are clichéd and hackneyed. My advice to you around the weakness question is that you should pick a weakness that isn't going to preclude you from the job and indicate how you've tackled that weakness and made improvements on it.

PANEL INTERVIEWS

An interview conducted by a panel of questioners as opposed to one conducted by an individual questioner usually happens at higher levels, where the post is CEO, head of department or – in the case of healthcare interviews – consultant. It's more daunting, because the interviewee has the feeling that they're facing a firing squad.

In fact, however, the task is the same. You have done your preparation and are determined to find opportunities to leave evidence of your relevant strengths with the panel. But although the task is the same, the structure, inevitably, will be different.

Typically, the panel will have divided up the questioning areas among them, so that each person covers a single topic or theme. If they're an ethical or professional team, they will have met well in advance of the interviews and decided on the competences to be adduced and the relative weightings to be attributed to each. It may, for example, be vital to prove, if you're going for a consultancy post as a cardio-thoracic surgeon, that you have done several by-pass operations and inserted dozens of stents in patients, whereas it may be less pivotal to be a strategic thinker. The panel may heavily weight the practical experience, laying a lighter weight on the capacity for strategic thinking, even though the latter would allow you to contribute to the day-to-day running of the hospital. If, on the other hand, you're going for a post as head of cardiology, strategic thinking may be more heavily weighted, as may people management, since it is the running of the entire department that is in question.

Most experienced panels have a deep understanding of employment and equality legislation and how it relates to the questions that they may ask. They may not ask a female candidate, for example, how she plans to manage the childcare issue her five offspring represent. Nor may they ask a single man or woman any question designed to elicit a statement about their sexual orientation. If, in any interview, you are asked a question related to your age, gender, sexual orientation, marital status, plans to have children or methods of taking care of existing children, you should gently point out that it isn't legal to ask you that question. But then move on to say something like, 'Of much more relevance to my performance in this job would be the fact that…' and offer some details of a past experience. That allows the board to recover from the horror of one of their members breaking the law and removes the paralysis of the error.

Towards the end of many interviews, an interviewer often asks one of two questions. The better of the two is: 'Is there anything that you haven't been asked that you wish you had been asked?'

Sometimes, this takes the form of an invitation to add anything that you feel would be relevant. Consider the question. Then either tell them that you believe the interview has been comprehensive and rigorous and that you don't have anything you need to add – or offer, clearly and decisively the extra information you want them to have, with a succinct explanation as to why you believe it to be relevant to their process.

The other question tends to be a variation on: 'Before we let you go, are there any questions you'd like to ask us?' Don't make one up. If you have a burning question, ask it. But ignore the people who say, 'Hey, Mick, make sure you ask something fierce clever about strategy. They'll think you're brainy.' Interview panels spot made-up questions. It'll be written all over you that you don't really give a hoot about the answer. So don't go there.

The other questions which should never be asked are the deadly twins:

- What are the details of the compensation package?
- When will I hear from you?

Remember the theme that has run through this entire chapter: the process is about solving the employer's problems, not yours. One of our client companies instantly disqualifies any job applicant who asks the question about the compensation package. They feel they have a superb reputation for paying people well and providing wonderful benefits and that any question which does not reflect that the interviewee knows this is insulting. The other question is just irritating in its assumption that if you don't nag them, they might be a bit slow in sending the letter of appointment to you.

In summary, at the point where the interviewer or interviewers go through the ritual of asking you if you have a question, offer one only if it demonstrates real interest in their company and is likely to be something they'll be happy to talk about – like, for example, the move of a pharmaceutical company into bio-pharm.

Discipline applied to this section of the interview is a courtesy to those asking the questions. Remember, interviewers are people too. By the time they get to asking, 'Have you any questions?' what they're really thinking is, 'Do I have enough time for a cup of coffee before the next victim?' Waste their coffee time at your peril. Arguably the best response to that question runs along the lines of, 'I feel I've done enough research at this stage and the interview has helped fill in the gaps. Thank you very much for the opportunity.' You should also have a 'closing pitch' prepared. Ask yourself: 'What's the last thing that I want this panel or interviewer to hear me say?' Prepare it. Rehearse it. And, on the day, when the right moment presents itself to you, say it.

The one person you need to be sure you're friendly to is your greeter or the receptionist. They often get asked their option of the candidate and if the response is, 'Seems OK,' rather than, 'A really nice person, very friendly,' you're screwed.

DOS AND DON'TS OF JOB INTERVIEWS

- Do prepare. Prepare to prove to the interview panel that you are the person for the job. Prepare examples that illustrate you doing the things they'll need you to do.
- Do research the company inside and out. You should have a clear understanding of the company's identity, the specific services or products they provide and how you would add value to the organisation. This takes more than going on to their website. Try newspaper sites or business sites. Or call a friend. In Ireland, you're never more than two people away from a useful contact who can give you a flavour of the company, as opposed to whatever you can glean from the mission or values statements on their

website. Don't be afraid to ask for information and help.

- Do dress professionally for your interview. Regardless of what the dress code is within an organisation (for example, business casual), an interview candidate should always look smart and professional. Proper business attire is necessary, not optional. Don't wear anything that is louder than you are.

- Do turn up early and if you are driving check out in advance where the parking is. You should aim to be there at least fifteen minutes before the starting time. Do your research on where to go and how to get there. Being late is more than a discourtesy: it raises questions over your general punctuality. These questions may not be fair, since the location may be one you've never had to go near before, but they'll nonetheless be raised in the minds of the interviewers. Worst of all, being late will send you into the interview panting, sweating and panicked. (Or, if you're female, panting, perspiring and panicked.)

- Do wash. This is important. Go in smelling of roses, but not too many roses. Stinking the room out with BO or some Eau de Posh won't do you any favours.

- Do use antiperspirant on your hands if you sweat profusely under pressure. Mitchum, the deodorant and antiperspirant people, do a good cream antiperspirant which can be rubbed into the palms of your hands to prevent clammy

dampness when you shake hands with the interviewer or interviewers.

- Don't talk money. You will appear as a mercenary and motivated by cash. The panel want you to be motivated by the desire to contribute to their business.
- Don't curse. Bad language in an interview is a complete no-no. Even if they do.
- Don't go out drinking the night before the interview. If you can't stay off the booze the night before an important interview, when can you?
- Don't forget it's your job to offer the information, not wait for them to drag it out of you. It's not an oral exam. The right question might not be asked. So be proactive with the information rather than reactive.

INDUSTRY VIEW: BRIAN HANRAHAN OF SENTENIAL
Sentenial is a quickly-expanding Irish software company. Brian Hanrahan, the company's business development director, believes that commitment to the job hunt is vital.

If you're applying for a 'thinking' role then adequately research the company and industry prior to your interview so you are able to pose insightful questions when requested. Having uninteresting, or worse still, no questions sometimes really lets candidates down you believed were strong until that very last impression. Don't be afraid to sell yourself. If I

as an interviewer suspect you might be a good candidate, don't force me to drag proof out through questioning; that only makes me doubt that initial impression.

If I've asked you to attend an interview then you can take it that I'm hoping you're the 'man' for the job. So when I ask questions assume I'm gathering evidence and give me as many examples as possible and don't restrict yourself to examples from one previous role when responding to direct questions.

Karl Manning, Director of Retail Sales at Halifax, believes preparation is key:

Fail to prepare, prepare to fail, as Roy Keane once said. I'm a big believer in preparation. There are only so many questions and themes that could possibly come up in an interview situation. Be sure to have these as well prepared as possible. It gives you the confidence going in the door that you're ready to answer what's thrown at you. Inevitably there will be one 'left of field' question that you wouldn't expect. But if you have every other possible scenario covered then you will feel much more relaxed about trying to answer this one.

I go into every interview hoping I will find someone that will blow me away. Interviewers want people to do well, to do themselves justice. I prefer to look at an interview as, 'I am there to

catch you on the things you're doing well and understand them,' as opposed to being there to 'catch you out'. Mind you, I will, if the person starts lying.

8

Presentations – at Interviews and at Work

Presentations in interviews offer a terrific opportunity to shine. You can communicate directly with the interview panel, face-to-face. (Our research shows that the second most effective mode of communication is face-to-face, to a small group. That's bettered only by talking face-to-face with one person.) You can demonstrate your familiarity with and connection to the company or organisation you want to join. You can display your powers of influencing and persuasion. You can – and this may be the best bit – remind them of your unique skills and achievements, the ones that show them you're the answer to their prayer.

Preparing for this presentation should follow the same course as for any other interview preparation. You ask yourself (about the interview panel): 'Who are these people? What have I to offer that may be of interest and use to them?' To those questions, add, 'What are their special concerns? How can I respond helpfully to them?' You have to be interesting, understandable and memorable while you meet all these requirements. Otherwise you won't have their full attention. You must secure that, if you are to make a strong impact on them.

Most interview panels are between two and four in number, although some, especially those for higher posts in the public service, can be larger. Some of the panels for hospital consultancy posts exceed ten – yes, ten – in number. However, most such interviews are preceded by one-to-one meetings between candidates and panel members, giving the candidate the chance to get a better understanding of the panel members' interests and concerns.

This is what you have to do, for any size of panel. First of all, find out who they are. Ring up the company and ask the HR manager or the person in charge of the recruitment process how the panel will be made up. Ask for the names and positions of the panel members.

There is another set of questions to ask – about the interviewers' enthusiasms, sore points and bottom lines, in other words, what they'd be prepared to go to the stake for. There's no point in presenting with fervent gusto the value of the social economy to a rabid capitalist who wouldn't know a volunteer if one came up and bit him on the leg. Don't try to use the presentation to change the interviewers' mind about anything – unless you think they've decided you shouldn't get the job.

Which raises the issue of when in the interview process the presentation happens. Some companies like you to present before the interview, some after. Some ask for a presentation only as part of a second interview. In this situation a presentation may assume greater importance, for two reasons. They may want it because they can't think of any other way to separate the gem from the other second-rounders. They may want it because, in their company, presentations form a huge part of their communication strategies and procedures. Either way, make the most of the chance you've been handed.

So, you've found out who the panel are and what makes them tick. Next, you have to ask yourself what you have to offer them. You want them to give you the job (your 'communication objective'), so what will you say that will convince them? Paradoxically, it's less about how wonderful you are and much more about how your unique skills will add value to their wonderful organisation. You need to know a lot about their organisation to be able to sell it enthusiastically back to them with yourself embedded in it.

To get them to the point where you want them, you must get them to remember you and the cool stuff about you. Here's an interesting fact. You must make the synapses in the brains of your listeners fire, in order to move something from short-term memory into long-term memory. When we get people to paint pictures in their heads, that's when the synapses fire. We have to help the interviewer with vivid examples, analogies and stories for them to remember what we're saying.

One of our clients, training with Terry Prone, began to give her an example. Terry said, 'Hold on, I know this story. This is the story of the little six-year-old who stopped going to school. She was OK on the days her mother was out at work, but on days she didn't work, the little girl had to find somewhere else to spend the day, no matter how wet or cold it was. Barnardos (the children's charity) heard about this and arranged for her to attend a breakfast club, where she could have a shower. That's why she had stopped going to school, because her classmates said she was smelly and wouldn't sit beside her or play with her. This was an example of how poverty affects children socially – not the obvious things like not having a good coat or nourishing food. How do I know this story?'

'Because I told it to you the last time I was here for training – eighteen months ago,' the client said. Terry's detailed recall, a year and a half later, was the result of a powerful story, well told. You'll note that not only was the story recalled, but the concept the story was meant to illustrate (the social effects of child poverty).

Story is one of the most effective ways of getting people to remember ideas. Small wonder, when we realise that's how people have been handing down beliefs, traditions and mores for hundreds of years. From Scandinavian sagas to Greek legends, every human group has its own stories – and reveres the storytellers – think of the special place the *seanchaí* had in Irish culture.

Significant in the Barnardos story, though, is the link with the audience's interests and concerns. This was a touching story about a child, engaging the listener's emotions. The more you can tap into emotions, the more you can engage people. As Stalin said, '30,000 soldiers killed in battle – that's a statistic. One child drowned in a pond – that's a tragedy.'

Another point was that the story was being told to a mainly female audience. Without being sexist, I have observed that women, by and large, identify with family and domestic examples. Men tend to use martial and sporting metaphors, like a level playing field and winning the battle for customers. Women talk about the recipe for success.

Now you can see another good reason for finding out about your interview panel. No point in telling a tear-jerker to a pressurised Chief Financial Officer, who is concerned about the company's viability. You will need to show her you can cut costs and bring in extra revenue with the ideas you have for new sales – through a vivid story of success, against the odds, in a previous role.

Think about the requirements of the role and how your skills, experiences and characteristics match them. Turn the cold facts into warm stories of achievement and ongoing learning. Warm stories because the interviewers need to see someone they can make a relationship with, someone who can fit into the organisation. And they need to know that you regard every experience as something to learn from. That's how they'll see you as being a long-term asset to them.

Confine yourself to three main points in your presentation, because our research shows that the most people take away from a presentation is three ideas – and sometimes only two or even one. This doesn't mean you only need three stories or examples. You need a number of illustrations, to cater for the different personalities and their diverse interests and concerns.

To give evidence of your people-management skills, you might need to tell them about the under-performing staff member who turned out to have an ongoing migraine problem and how you arranged for him to have regular brief times off for treatment. The outcome: a healthy and productive worker. This story might well mesh with the approach of the female HR manager on the panel. By contrast, the male Chief Operations Officer might need to hear about your uncompromising tactics in dealing with an unpunctual repeat offender. In giving them both stories, you're displaying your versatility and hitting the spot with at least two of the panel.

When deciding what your three main ideas are, think about the elements of the job description and the person specification that seem crucial. Talk to someone who knows the company well about the company, its ethos and internal climate.

Now you must make your three key ideas interesting, understandable and memorable, by using the most vivid examples and the strongest evidence you can find. Remember any claim you make is no more compelling than anyone else's – until you give evidence, in the form of great examples.

End with a one-sentence summary of the great match you are with the company, evidenced by a short précis of how the learning from your previous experiences could make a huge difference in adding value to their organisation.

When you present to them, start with a smile. Daniel Goleman, author of *Emotional Intelligence*, highlights research findings about smiling in mammals and especially humans. As well as making the smiler feel better, a consequence of being smiled at is that people are likely to smile back, thus making them feel better. You therefore start with a more relaxed presenter and listeners.

Make eye contact with each member of the panel. This establishes an initial connection with them and helps you in your task of keeping them listening. (You need to be interesting too, of course.) When you look at the panel, you'll get feedback about how you're doing. Smiles and nods are encouraging signs that you're maintaining their interest and making a good impression. Frowns of puzzlement may indicate that you need to go back and explain that last bit again.

Speak in short sentences. Use simple words, so everyone stays with you. When we don't understand something in a written piece, we can go back and reread it. We can't do that when we're listening, so don't have anyone wondering what you mean by 'quotidian'. They'll go off in their heads trying to figure it out. While they do, they're no longer listening to you. Use the word 'daily' or 'commonplace' instead. If they can't understand something, they certainly can't remember it. To make them remember your claims, relate the kind of vivid stories and examples we recommended earlier – they are also your evidence, the proof of your claims.

If this presentation has been at the beginning of the interview process, wait for the interviewers to set up the next steps. That's also the drill for the presentation at the second interview.

If the presentation is at the end of your interview, you have a chance to repair any damage done, or fill in any gaps in the interview itself. You can incorporate the convincing examples of a specific skill that you left out earlier. You can subtly correct any misunderstanding that you believe may have occurred in some of the questioning. End with energy and impact.

Most panels or interviewers will have questions during or after the presentation. Prepare for these as an integral part of your presentation groundwork. Figure out what the obvious questions are – I mean the obvious questions from their point of view. Prepare answers (don't forget your evidence) for each of them. Then think of the questions you pray you won't get asked – the nasties. Prepare for them too. Figuring out these answers will probably help you to craft your presentation more persuasively and will certainly give you confidence facing into the presentation.

Including the answers to as many questions as possible in the presentation content is the ideal. But be careful, in doing this, that you don't exceed the time allowed. Hitting the allocated time-slot shows professionalism and respect for the panel. Leaving one or two 'hooks' to prompt questions from the panel may be best way of dealing with more complex issues. They give you the opportunity to tease these out in discussion, establishing further links with the panel – developing almost a collaborative approach.

When questions are over, thank them; check what the next steps are; smile; say goodbye and leave; or sit down and wait for the interview.

PRESENTATIONS AT WORK: CAREER DEVELOPMENT OR CAREER DEATH?

'You did a great job on the gibbon project,' your boss says. 'I want you to give a presentation on it to the middle-management group next week.'

What's your reaction? Delighted anticipation? Abject fear? Or blank puzzlement, as in: why the middle-management group? Why next week? Why me?

If it's the last few of these, ask her. You need to know what her expectations are: of you *and* of the presentation. Ask what she wants the middle-management group to get out of it. Does she want them to do anything as a result? Does she want them to do anything differently as a result? What's the relevance of the timing? Are you to make a case for expanding production of gibbons? Will they need financials? And of course, how long is it to be? Where? At what time? Is it part of a longer meeting? Who else will be presenting? If so, who'll be going ahead of you and who'll be following you?

These are the kinds of questions you need to ask about any work presentation assigned to you, whether it excites you or fills you with dread. You need to get a full and clear picture of your boss's expectations or those of whoever asked you to do it. After all, the motives of a colleague may not be as pure as the driven snow.

We worked some time back with a company that fostered a relentlessly competitive culture among their staff. When one of them had a presentation to make that he perceived as a poisoned chalice, he would try to offload it on to an unsuspecting peer, who would then be savaged with nasty questions from other staff who'd been lying in the long grass waiting for an opportunity to have a go at anyone from the HR (or wherever – fill in from your own experience) section. If you work in that kind of context and culture, for your own self-protection you need to be very clear on the outcome required by the person asking you to make the presentation and by the people present.

Being asked to do a presentation doesn't mean they're out to get you but it pays to understand why you're being asked. In some companies presentations now substitute for the inter-office memo. (Whatever happened to them?) In other words, presentations are how information is shared. Just make sure it's important information and make it worth your listeners' while to sit and listen to you for twenty minutes, because preparation for a presentation begins with listeners: Who are they? What do they know about your topic? Why are they attending? What have you got that may be of interest to them?

Keep in mind the iron law of all communications: people pay attention to and remember only what:

- Threatens/affects them
- Benefits them
- Interests them

I've started the list with negatives because a threat is arguably the most effective way of grabbing attention. The biggest corporate bang comes from communicating something that will have or may have negative implications for people working in your company or organisation. Once they get past the threat, they will pick up likely benefits. If they travel that far with you, their interest will be kept by your presentation connecting with something or someone they know about or have an interest in.

The biggest single switch-off for an audience is the growing awareness that what you are saying has no relevance to them. At the very least, you should create a reaction of passing interest, the result of surprise: 'I haven't heard that before...' or, 'I haven't heard it put that way before...'

The next biggest boredom-creating factor is data overload. This usually happens when you're very nervous. You go into survival mode – 'I'll give them everything I know – that will fill the twenty minutes.' But will they get anything useful out of it?

In planning a presentation you have to decide how many new ideas or propositions an audience can absorb, internalise and make their own while listening to you. The number does not expand with the length of your presentation. The consensus of psychological researchers and academics studying what people pick up from presentations is that it is unlikely that listeners can process any more than two or three new ideas. Identify and present the two or three thoughts that will have most impact on and relevance to your target audience. When you have decided what these are, spend the bulk of your time creating illustrations and vivid examples calculated to make those ideas come alive for the audience and become memorable to them. At least twice as much time should be spent on *how* you will make your points relevant and memorable as on *what* are the points you are going make.

Here's a useful tip. When you are preparing a presentation, ask yourself these two questions:

- Would I say this if I were speaking to a member of the audience on a one-to-one basis?
- Would I say it this way if I were speaking to a member of the audience on a one-to-one basis?

If the answer to one or both these questions is *no*, then you should not be including the idea or describing it the way you are in your presentation.

With the gibbon presentation, some of the questions you should ask yourself might include:

- What do the middle-management group need to hear about it?
- What is their current level of knowledge about the project?
- What aspects of it are different?
- What would be useful for them to hear about: your development method?; your pricing process?; your marketing approach?
- In other words, how can you help them?

Once you have focused your presentation on the real needs of your listeners, have thought of stories and examples to bring that home to them and are sure you are not going to overload them with 'stuff', you must then put your ideas into a storyline that will be easy to follow. The presentation must have a clear structure – a beginning, a middle and an end. It must have a strong introduction and conclusion and a running theme linking it all together.

This is the point at which you ask yourself if the ideas in your presentation would be more easily assimilated by the audience if you used some visuals. This does not mean devising a set of text-based slides. Visual aids are to help your audience to understand. So the best visual aid is you, since you can check for their understanding throughout the presentation. If you use visuals to support your talk, remember that your most effective aid would be a live object that your audience can clearly see. For example, mechanical engineers encouraging school students to enrol in a particular college bring a real replacement hip with them to give the students a practical example of how all kinds of problems are solved by engineers.

Then the order of priority would be:

1. Pictures
2. Artist's impressions
3. Diagrams, histograms, pie charts, flow charts
4. Selected statistics in tabular form
5. Text with meaning and significance, for example, quotations or definitions
6. Bullet-point text, usually as a summary

An academic named Edward Tufte, Professor Emeritus at Yale University, undertook an in-depth study of the cognitive properties of PowerPoint bullet-point text, called *The Cognitive Style of PowerPoint: Pitching Out Corrupts Within*. He concluded that PowerPoint was:

- Presenter-friendly
- Content/significance-destructive
- Audience-distracting

As Professor Tufte points out, you can't read and listen effectively at the same time. So why distract your audience by giving them conflicting tasks? When they're looking at a slide, they're not looking at or listening to you. You're losing your best weapons of persuasion and influence – your face, voice and words.

If you decide to use slides, keep them visual. The easiest way to check the quality of a slide is to ask yourself, 'Does this visual explain something in a way I couldn't?' Tell people in advance of each slide a little about why they're seeing it. Then show it to them – and stop talking while they take it in. Then talk about it, right up at the screen if at all possible, and add value to what they're seeing.

A useful device to control audience focus, when you're finished with a slide, is to blank the screen, so you have everyone's full attention. To blank the screen, hit the letter B on the keyboard. To reactivate for the next slide, hit B again and move to the next slide.

Practising your presentation
Now, say your presentation out loud in a room on your own.

Not in front of a mirror. A mirror distracts you with your own mannerisms and appearance. And you're not your audience. If you have a compliant friend or colleague, you may find it useful to present to them. Even saying it to yourself highlights the sentences that are too long, the jargon that no one but you and your peers understand and the links that are giving you difficulty.

Before you deliver any presentation publicly, you should be verbally familiar with it, not just conceptually familiar. As you talk it through, pay particular attention to the junctions and transitions between themes and ideas. They're the trickiest bit of any presentation: as you move from one point to the next you run the highest risk of getting muddled – and if you get lost in your links, you can bet your audience will too.

Be wary of writing out your presentation. Most of us, when we sit down at a keyboard, write the written rather than the spoken language. If a presentation is written for the written rather than the spoken word it will be difficult to deliver and it will be heard as at best clunky and at worst portentous and obscure.

Every time you encounter a human being, however fleetingly, as well as exchanging information you are also building or unbuilding a relationship. This happens all the time that you are making a presentation. So you must figure out some of the elements that make your personal impact on your listeners – your overall deportment, your body language as you deliver, your eye-contact with the audience (if you're using PowerPoint, don't spend your time looking at the screen or your lap-top), the ease within yourself that you transmit to others. Relationships are built with an audience who get a sense that the deliverer owns the presentation. Your presentation must not be simply the process of transferring bones from one grave to another.

If you need to persuade people to follow a specific course of action, you must be convinced of its efficacy yourself. You won't be able to influence anyone else to do something you wouldn't do yourself. Passion carries considerable impact. But passion on its own, unrelated to the needs of an audience, can be counter-productive. Take, for example, the passion displayed by the Hungarian medic, Ignaz Semmelweiss (1818-65), in trying to put an end to childbed fever. Semmelweiss found the link between autopsies and huge numbers of maternal deaths. He worked out that the surgeons were bringing something on their unwashed hands, directly from the corpses they autopsied, and inserting that something into the bodies of women at the point of delivering babies, thereby infecting them with puerperal fever, a lethal disease. Unfortunately his tactic was to accuse – passionately – his consultant colleagues of murder. Not surprisingly he made no converts and ended his life in an asylum. He was right, but it took many years and a much more conciliatory approach before the research of French microbiologist Louis Pasteur (1822-95) into germs brought about changes in hospital procedures and practice.

When it comes to presentations, many of us worry about our delivery. Some of the comments trainers have heard from course participants over the years include: 'My voice is very monotonous,'; 'I'm saying "em" a lot,'; even, 'I'm boring myself.' The interesting thing is when you're concerned about your audience, when you use concrete examples to help them understand the concepts you're explaining, when you construct your presentation into a coherent story-line and when you can talk to the audience convincingly using your own experiences – suddenly the delivery takes care of itself.

This happens because your focus is them, not yourself; because concrete examples and a storyline not only bring the presentation to life and help to move the ideas into long-term memory, but keep your own interest and engagement – because you speak with conviction. For all these reasons your delivery becomes animated, personal, energetic and enthusiastic. Above all, when you're not constrained by reading text off slides and just talk to people, your communication will be more real. Try it and see.

These are the key elements to all presentations:

- Audience focus
- Creation of understanding
- Structure
- Personal ownership
- Delivery

The good news is that following all the advice detailed above removes 90 per cent of the fear. Doing your presentation this way leaves you with great eye contact with your audience, always valuable in relating to them, a much simpler communication task and an easily-followed preparation method. People can actually enjoy presenting. And once you enjoy it, it's much more likely to advance your career, rather than do it mortal damage.

NERVES
The symptoms of nerves – wet hands, trembling hands, a desire to throw up, a need to go to the toilet, blanking, perspiring – are all indicators of adrenalin pouring into your

system. Adrenalin is the 'fight or flight' hormone that helped our primeval ancestors to survive a meeting with a bear. In a nano second, while their brain worked out the options – run like hell or stab the bear in the jugular – adrenalin pumped into their bloodstream to ensure that when they made their decision, whether it was to leg it or stab the grizzly, they could do it. Adrenalin makes you think faster and more clearly. It gives an urgency and excitement to what you're saying that might otherwise be absent. It makes you slightly larger than life. All of which is good for a presentation and a job interview. I work with an ex-boxer named Sam Storey, a big, strong, tough fellow from Belfast.

'Were you ever nervous going into a fight?' I asked him.

'For God's sake, if I wasn't nervous, I'd be worried,' was Sam's reply.

Nerves are a necessary accompaniment of public speaking and persuasion. So if you are presenting in work, or in an interview, don't worry when the nerves come.

What causes people real trouble though, are the symptoms of nerves – the outward and visible manifestation of adrenalin pumping through your system. Learn to cope with those symptoms. Excessive sweating, for example, is manageable – use a really good antiperspirant. Don't wear shirts that will show maps of Europe appearing under each armpit. If you find your hands are sweaty, a bit of talc can dry them up, or dry them on your trousers before you shake someone's hand.

Another symptom is a tremor in your hands. Holding a script or cards when your hands are trembling is difficult. The pages will flap, you'll fan the front row of the audience and it will be patently obvious to everyone that you're nervous. Long before AutoCue, the BBC newsreaders had to hold the pages of their script up in order to have them in their eyeline. Many of them found that their hands shook. Someone in there taught them a preventative measure (it does work, I know this because I do it) consisting of clenching your hands as tightly and strongly as possible for forty-five seconds to a minute. The newsreaders were taught to do this in the sixty seconds prior to going on air. When the 'On Air' light would go on, they'd release their hands and pick up their script. Their hands wouldn't shake for the rest of the broadcast.

Another piece of advice is to talk before an interview. Most people prior to an interview or presentation sit in silence. They don't speak to anybody. But like a singer or a sportsperson, you need to warm up. My cousin, *Dragon's Den* star Gavin Duffy, has a rhyme, 'Rubber baby, buggy bumper, moving up and down.' He goes through this aloud before any session, particularly in the morning, to warm up his voice. Before your interview, rather than starting to rhyme things to yourself, chat to the receptionist. It will get you talking and make a good impression on him or her which they may pass on to the interviewer.

One of the most predictable side effects of the arrival of adrenalin into the bloodstream is dry-mouth syndrome. Suddenly, your mouth and tongue are like sandpaper. So before you start your interview or presentation, be sure to have a glass of water with you.

If you fumble over a word or make a mistake in the interview, don't beat yourself up about it, because it happens to everyone, they probably won't remember it and you'll lose focus. 'Keep her lit' is my motto.

Blanking is the single biggest worry for everyone. It actually isn't blanking. It's overload. With adrenalin running through you, your brain can process more thoughts in a split second than it could normally do. This is great, because you can think faster. However, it can also have a negative affect. Blanking can come from doing a running post mortem on your interview or presentation as you go. Wrong thing to be doing. Focus. If blanking does happen, the solution is not to make the audience uncomfortable. Just announce that you've blanked. The vast majority of audiences and panels will understand it. And help you out. They'll give you a name if you can't remember it, or they'll steer you back to what you were talking about.

9

PAY REVIEWS AND NEGOTIATIONS – BECAUSE YOU'RE WORTH IT

The first thing you must realise, as you embark on your career, is that a performance review actually starts a year before you have it.

'No performance assessment without performance agreement,' is how our chairman Tom Savage sums it up. Tom pioneered Performance Management Development Systems (PMDS) within the Irish civil service and has always laid huge emphasis on this basic point: that people must know what they're supposed to be doing before they can be measured on it. The fact that they can contribute to an assessment at the end of a year's work doesn't make it a fair assessment if it wasn't made clear to them at the outset what they were supposed to be doing.

This message hasn't got through to many companies, with the result that the biggest mistake they make when it comes to reviewing the performance of their staff is to judge them on criteria that the staff never knew were in play. When this happens someone who thinks they're playing a blinder goes into a performance review and discovers a list of things that – in the eyes of the people to whom they report – they've been failing to do. They had no awareness of this list before the assessment started and even less awareness that they were failing on it. What's worse, when this happens, the employee frequently learns that the things they thought they were succeeding on are regarded by their management as irrelevant.

This should never happen. It creates a false expectation and great disappointment on both sides and by the time a shared understanding is achieved, it may be too late to undo the damage done. Remember, in this scenario it's not through lack of effort that the person has not done well. It's simply that they didn't know their own assessment criteria. So if you know you are going to have a performance review in three months, six months, nine months or twelve months, you should immediately ensure that you have total clarity as to the criteria on which you are going to be reviewed. Only then can you know what you should prioritise. Never mind what *you* would like to prioritise as this may not be measured in management terms at all.

The second thing is that there is no zero option. Everyone gets reviewed on the basis of some criteria whether or not they know what they are. We were once with a client in a firm who said, 'We don't want any of this performance management stuff.'

It sounded very clear and direct and no messing.

'But everybody employed here is currently assessed, whether or not they know it,' we said.

'Nonsense,' they said.

'Every company, every boss assesses the performance of their staff all the time,' we pointed out. 'They may not do it officially or overtly; they do it, nonetheless. Every boss makes judgements about the people working for him or her. These judgements could be based on you showing up on time or being constantly late. They could be based on the colour of your shoes, whether you smile or present a grave face to the world, how quickly you react to instructions and how much care you take over projects given to you to complete. It doesn't matter. At the end of the year someone will look at an employee's performance over the past twelve months and make a decision about whether or not he gets a bonus or a raise. You can do it in an arbitrary, unacknowledged way, or you can do it in a way you share with your employees and that they fully understand and buy into.'

Older bosses, who have run extremely successful companies based on their personal reactions to the performance of employees, always have some arbitrary criteria on which they base promotion or bonus or raise-in-income decisions and can be most reluctant to – as they see it – swap a fair and effective system for a more bureaucratic version which lessens their personal power. That's their choice. But it's a choice which, for their own safety, should be clearly incorporated into the contract of employment they offer anybody coming to work for them. If you're going to work for such a company, be clear that you will have no measures by which you can work out how to shine and be promoted. You'll have to read the runes and do educated guesswork. (Of course, that kind of boss will immediately, reading what I've just written, claim that someone who can read the runes, do educated guesswork and bloody well get on with it is exactly the person they want to employ.)

A more systematic approach to performance briefing and assessment can be easier on both sides and more productive for both sides. In any situation where there's a bonus, where there's a salary raise, where people are making judgements about how you did, the best position to be in is one in which a clear agreement is in place whereby you understand the basis for all judgements made about you.

If there isn't a good formal performance management system in place you need to go and find out what the boss is actually looking for from you and the key things that they're judging your performance on. Or, better still, push them into putting such a system in place. I was recently in a company which had been set up in the teeth of a recession, staffed by people who had all recruited each other, because they were friends. One of the staff, at the end of the first year, insisted on being assessed by her boss. Because they were friends, because they were busy, because it was an informal culture, the boss fought it as long as he could. Then caved in. And announced immediately afterwards that it was the best thing he'd done in years, because he had learned things about his company he needed to learn and had heard what he described as 'brilliant proposals' from an employee who was usually too snowed under by the minutiae of her day to propose policy changes.

The feeling of bureaucracy about performance reviews puts many people off. They don't like yet another bit of paper going into the system about them, or having to fill in forms that decide whether or not they meet the requirements of some externally-applied 'balanced score card'. They hate what they feel are 'official' conversations with questions like: 'What are your goals and objectives, long-term, medium-term and short-term?' No aspect of management needs to be this boring and dehumanised. Good organisations have a simple framework that establishes what staff should be praised for and rewarded for and what behaviours are corporately unacceptable? When this shared understanding underpins the setting of a few goals (I'm sorry, I had to use that word once) for you as an individual staffer, you know you're not being processed by a big uncaring system but observed by people who want you to do the best you can do and be the best you can be.

When you're facing into your review, you should know, long before your boss tells you, how well you did in any area of your work, because you will have sat down and mentally assessed yourself through his or her eyes. If you want them to understand better than you suspect they do just how well you did in any particular aspect of the job, work out how you can show evidence for each strength you want to claim: evidence of each strength in action. Strengths can include fixing problems, predicting problems or coming up with new ideas.

Performance reviews must be more than checklists of what was achieved against what have been identified as aims. When it becomes a box-ticking exercise that happens every year and that bosses and staff alike hate having to go through, it's a faulty review system. Review systems should be part of the day-to-day appreciative development of potential among the employees, not a list-making process that sees the employee, like a hamster, taking successes and stuffing them in their cheeks to use at some (defensive) stage in the future.

A manager will form an opinion the same way anyone does – on a ongoing rolling basis throughout the year. This is stated at the review. If you have had mighty successes during the year, you should find an appropriate way to make sure the manager understands them. Too often, this notification process fails to inform the performance review. 'It's up to the boss to keep their eye on things and know what I'm doing,' some workers say.

This is the sure road to disappointment and the bigger the organisation, the more bitter the disappointment because the boss simply may not have the time or capacity to take notes about each individual employee's success rate. More seriously, if you ever find yourself saying something along these lines, stop it right there. It derives from a view of other people as responding to a collectively understood set of duties and responsibilities: what have been called the 'shoulds.' Human beings are notoriously averse to delivering on the 'shoulds' and if you build your expectation of personal career progress on a conviction that other people *should* do something, you will be constantly disappointed.

You should be going back regularly to your boss and saying, 'Just to let you know I talked to your man. Interesting what you said to me the last day. Got it. He's now buying, so sales are looking good.' This kind of ostensibly casual heads-up is in fact a report – an informal report on what you're doing and how effective you're being. The boss is getting that report well in advance of the performance review meeting – at a time when it can inform their thinking.

When you then get to the point of the meeting, before you start planning what you're going to say and what you're going to look for, look at it from the manager's point of view. Currently, in smaller companies and professional services companies, because of the external circumstances and market pressures, companies cannot generate the level of profits that would allow distribution of any form of reward among the staff. But you will still encounter staff members who cannot look at the situation except though the lens of their own expectations. 'I've been working very hard,' they say, furiously. 'I should get a bonus.'

'Yes and if I had wings I would be an angel,' may be the only answer. You can't be given something if it doesn't exist and getting bitter about not getting it can destroy relationships where you work. You will be in much greater control of a performance review meeting if first of all you get a realistic sense of where, precisely, the company is on all its objectives. If it's failing on all of its objectives while you're meeting all of yours, a disconnect exists, but sulking about it won't help your future within that firm.

The other factor you need to take into account before you go into a performance review is how realistic your self-appraisal is. Is it possible, for instance, that you rate yourself more highly than your employer does? It can help to ask yourself some blunt questions:

- I may have come up mightily but am I the top performer in here?
- He has six staff under him. How important am I to the business and to his particular division?
- What is he trying to achieve with this in-centivisation?
- Why do I have the feeling he doesn't appreciate how hard I work?
- Is my salary in line with other salaries in the market?
- Am I pushing my luck? Is it possible they might see me as already being over-paid?

- 'How exactly do they structure my salary?'

The salary structure varies widely between industrial sectors. Some people are paid on a metric of the business they generate outside the company. For example, legal firms work out that their staff should be pulling in three times their salary.

Some people, for example those working in an accountancy company, have a structure whereby their external billings are directly related to their pay.

Some people are paid a small salary and then a commission based on sales.

Each of these systems is affected in different ways by deteriorating economic times. But they're also influenced by personal performance. Let's say you work in an accountancy partnership and, up to recently, didn't have great relationships with clients. Now you've radically improved your listening skills and have developed enough confidence to be listened to and respected by them. That's a clear improvement. However, if your pay is based on billable hours, your boss may not offer you an improved salary commensurate with this aspect of your improved performance.

'Aidan, you're mighty,' she may tell you. 'Last year you kept spitting in the eye of clients and I was constantly getting complaining phone calls about you. This year, they're ringing me saying you're the best guy they ever met. However, you haven't actually earned a penny more. So all I can do is give you lots of praise and support for the marvellous change you have achieved. But I can't give you money out of a pool that you haven't created.'

You may be and no doubt will be furious. But you have

to understand the process from the manager's perspective. If you're heading into a salary negotiation you need to scope out what you believe is a reasonable end position both for you and your boss.

People go into formal pay negotiations as if they were a random horse-trade or haggling in a Moroccan bazaar. You shouldn't. Negotiations should be about mutual gain, not one-upmanship. It's not about just getting the best deal for yourself but about getting the best for both parties. The thing that you need to be clear about in salary negotiation is that salary is future tense, bonus is past tense. If you're looking for a bonus, you're trying to prove that the salary you were paid last year does not equate to the delivery that was achieved in return for that salary. For example, the boss pays you €50,000, but in actual fact you sold €75,000 worth of stuff. In the negotiations with your boss, I'd be pointing out this piece of evidence.

For salary raises it's not just a case of looking at last year's performance. You have to prove you're consistently improving and contributing more to the company's successes. You need to have a small bit of future tense stuff that says, 'Those kinds of sales that are coming in, I can see another four of them,' or, 'That success that I had in R and D – I have a further three projects of that kind.' You're trying to show how an investment in you in the future (the future salary) will be paid back by virtue of the stuff you will be doing.

You then need to approach a pay review in the way you would approach any negotiation, by asking yourself:

- What is my ultimate aim?
- What do I want?

- What am I going to ask for?
- What is my minimum position? (the point under which I am going to say to myself, 'I'm looking for another job as this is now an insult.')
- What are the points of compromise that I could establish? Employees tend to go in with a hard number in their head and say, 'Pay me X'. Then the boss tends to say no and the whole thing dissolves.

If you go in and say, 'I think I'm worth X,' and they say 'Well, we think you're worth Y,' it can turn into a pointless ping-pong argument of the kind you might have in a mart in Offaly with two farmers haggling over a bull.

You haggle price with evidence around each assertion. The management might be saying, 'We know that was a roaring success. But we can't guarantee those sales for next year. I think that may be a bit excessive.' And on an evidence basis you're narrowing the gap between the two numbers and at a certain point that narrowing will stop. This may be because the boss has rolled over and played dead and said, 'We'll give you whatever you like.' It may be because you've rolled over and played dead and said, 'It's not worth the candle, I'll just accept it.' But if it has come to a point where the boss is at his maximum and you are at your minimum, what you need to have is clarity about the things in the middle that you can shift around. For example, 'How about paying for my VHI or my mobile phone?' or 'How about I get a parking space?'

There are many things in executive salaries that people don't recognise as being a direct benefit. You should have a few of these in mind so you can say, 'OK, I don't want to push you any further than I have, but a big difficulty for me is that I'm making a ton of work calls on my mobile phone and it's costing me a small fortune. Is there any chance you could pick that up?' People rarely think of benefits when they are negotiating salary but they are just as real as a raise and in some cases have a much lower cost to the company. For example, if the company wanted to give you €1,000 extra in your salary there would be PRSI implications. But if they pay your mobile phone bill of €1,000, it costs them €1,000 and it's €1,000 into your pocket. All these little points of compromise are very useful.

The other thing you want to make sure of in meetings like this is that you are not at a point of emotional confrontation. There shouldn't be any emotion in it. It's the manager's job to keep costs as low as he or she possibly can because that's the reality of how companies operate. Any company that says, 'Hey, cash for everyone,' is not going to be around for very long. Managers are just doing their job. On the other hand it's naturally in your interest to maximise your earnings. Neither of you is trying to shaft the other.

You shouldn't be going in braced for conflict. 'This is terribly emotionally fraught, but they're not going to beat me, I'll fight them to the death,' is not a good attitude to have at the start of any negotiation. You should also be making sure that you can support any claim with evidence, so that you're not just going in to beg or plead or demand.

Your approach should be: 'I can justify all this. This is the salary that is in the market; this is what I can get elsewhere; this is what I have done; this is what you said to me last year.' And you should say it in an extremely pleasant way.

The meeting should be very real, very frank and unemotional. You should not be combative. 'Well, OK, if we can't come to direct agreement,' you may find yourself saying, 'What are the points of compromise we can find here?'

Note that I've used the plural, collective, 'we'. Remember that if you turn it into a 'you versus them' situation, it is unlikely to help the negotiation and even less likely to help your future working relationship. It should always be a 'we', because, in addition to immediate concrete deliverables that you'd like to get out of any salary negotiation or performance review, if you manage it well you can emerge from the encounter feeling better about your relationship with your manager rather than worse, knowing that they have a clearer picture of what you contribute to the business.

In a recession the pot is generally empty and if the company does not have cash to pay out in salary increases, you're not going to get an increase, no matter how brilliantly you have performed in the previous twelve months.

Taking a salary reduction is a different issue and a much trickier issue, because we now have in Ireland a generation of younger people who knew only the good times; who made large amounts of money in certain industries. They are now being told by their bosses that salaries are coming down by 25 per cent. Because many of them have never experienced any of this before they're not very clear on employment law and they are simply saying OK. The reality is that your salary cannot be reduced without your express consent. Therefore, if you are being asked to take a salary review or a salary reduction it must come with some gain to you, the employee. It's the reverse of the process described earlier. You may need to do some research, especially if you do not totally trust the management ethos of the company for which you work. I have seen a number of appallingly unjust salary reductions in some companies, which were accepted because people knew no better, but which, in the longer term, will do the companies involved enormous damage because the employees who took the salary cuts realise that they're not contributing to the economy as much as they're contributing to the company's owners keeping their villa in France. Any manager who doesn't beginning the conversation by saying, 'I'm taking twice the cut I'm asking you to take – now let us discuss…' should be challenged.

The second aspect of accepting a salary cut is the future planning dependent upon it.

'I accept a cut of a quarter in my salary,' you may tell them. 'That means my living conditions are going to be 25 per cent worse for the next year. I accept that. Now I need to know – and have in writing from you – what happens when there is an upturn in the economy? When does my salary return to its current level? Does that happen in a similar way for all staff? What bonus do I get? Is there a way I can be linked to company profit targets so that if we do grow a profit, in two years' time I get a certain amount back? Is there a way to ensure my position for a longer period of time?' You need to be thinking: 'How do I protect myself?'

For instance if I was in an industry with a large numbers of employees in my division and I was asked to take a 25 per cent pay cut as a function of that, I would want a promise that I would not be made redundant. If there was a potential redundancy I would need to maximise my earnings up to the point where I am let go. If they're saying I have to take a 25 per cent pay cut I would make a contract with them that I keep my job as long as this company is afloat. If they are saying, 'You're going to take a 25 per cent cut,' I want an official piece of paper saying that as soon as the company gets profitable some of the profit comes to me rather than simply going to management. I want a contract that indicates that this is a short-term measure due to be reversed on such a date. Otherwise I am into a rolling series of negotiations to get back to where I was two years ago – which is a lot of faith to put in management. If you know and trust the company, what they offer may be reasonably acceptable, but it's likely to be much less acceptable coming from managers who you know have already made bad decisions.

One aspect of performance reviews that is extremely challenging is demonstrating good behaviour outside the sections which can be measured. It is very easy to prove that sales improved on your watch and within your area of responsibility. It is now becoming common, however, for managers to articulate at the beginning of the year a list of competences that they wish you to improve on. One of the biggest difficulties is how to prove that you have improved on any one of these competences. How, for example, can you prove that you were better at teamwork during the past year than you were the year before? How do you prove yourself better at the communications competence?

It's a little like an ongoing job interview, in which you have to give examples to prove that you are good in a particular area, with the added complication that you must break it down so that you have a reasoned response when your manager says, 'Billy, I'm not sure that you are actually great at the teamwork bit.'

'In fact, I saw Mairéad last week crying in the corner because she was so overworked,' you may reply, 'I helped her calm down and I took away half the tasks she was worried about and sorted them out for her. In addition, I saw Joe sitting at a meeting two weeks ago and it was obvious to me that he was completely baffled as to what was going on and was too scared to ask. I went and briefed him afterwards so he was able to pick up and confidently deliver for all of us. In addition, when I am in charge of meetings, I'm very good at making sure everybody's clear and committed to whatever emerges as the most urgent issue. I'm sure, Frank, that you would agree that each of these is a good example of teamwork in action.'

If Frank wants to hang on to an unevidenced prejudice against you, you can prevent this by gently insisting that he gives you specifics: examples to prove that you are not good at teamwork. If he comes up with a couple of good examples, don't fight it. Consider what he has said and indicate that you understand the examples he has cited might add up, in his view, to poor teamwork. But then set them against the examples of positive teamwork you have already given him. Don't get emotionally involved. Talk about yourself as confidently and dispassionately as if you were talking about a third party.

What executives regularly discover in this context is that the manager gets woolly if he or she has not prepared for the meeting in advance (and too many managers fail to prepare properly for performance reviews) and then tends to back off. Impressionistic old guff doesn't stand up to calm interrogation and hard evidence.

In some companies there are performance management systems that seem quite insane. These involve looking at human interactions as if there were mechanical processes.

One company I worked for had a performance assessment for call-centre staff whereby the length of time they spent on the phone in the call centre was a measure of how successful they were because it showed how quickly you had solved the customer's problem. It took management a year to work out that when staff knew they had a four-minute cut-off target, when they reached 3 minutes 30 seconds they'd say to the customers, 'I'll ring you back in two seconds,' hang up the phone and start a new call. So although the problem took twelve minutes to fix, it looked like three four-minute conversations. Customers thought it was nuts and it took a long time to work through the system. Companies are discovering that this is not the kind of management system that will get the best out of employees.

One last thing: your attitude to the performance assessment will contribute a lot to how the meeting goes. You may have thought and thought and rehearsed. You may have worked yourself up to the point of: 'What if I don't get it?; What if she says this?; What if she does that?' If you are thinking like this you are looking for a reason to row or to be proven wrong. You will be up to ninety, wound like a spring. The meeting will have a really tense start, with people quickly getting into binary opposition and the whole thing turning sour. Once you have done your mental preparation, go in assuming the best and if it turns out otherwise, fine. Prepare mentally for a good outcome: this means you are far more likely to go into the meeting sunny and upbeat. Everyone will be at ease and you will get to the negotiation in a friendly way. If you wind yourself up thinking about what the negatives are likely to be, both sides will very quickly be stuck in hard-line positions.

10

Communicating in the Workplace

'Every time you open your mouth, you are either building or unbuilding a relationship.'
Tom Savage, Chairman, the Communications Clinic

This is true in every relationship but especially in the workplace. In order to develop your career with your current employer your communication skills are vital. Research has found that roughly eight out of ten workplace failures can be attributed to bad communication. Even if you are technically superb, even if you are punctual, punctilious and a perfectionist, you may not even survive, let alone develop in the job, without excellent communication and relationship skills. There are four areas you need to watch for when communicating.

- Your ability to listen
- Your ability to present your point of view empathetically
- Your ability to trade and negotiate
- Your ability to handle conflict and/or criticism when it happens

YOUR ABILITY TO LISTEN

A key element in your communication and relationship-building skill is your ability to listen. The vast majority of people reckon they're great listeners. They're not. Failure to listen blocks information at source. Information, in terms of developing your career, is vital. Bad listening skills will cause you difficulty around completing projects, because you won't get the brief right. They will cause you difficulty with customers, because you'll miss the important information that indicates what they really want. Becoming a good listener is the best step you can take in communication terms. It will not only make you better at your job, it will turn you into a better friend, improve your relationship with your spouse or partner and greatly improve your performance as a team member.

There are three types of listening:

- Listening to talk – the bore does this.
- Listening to win – the competitor does this.
- Listening to understand – the listener does this.

Shy people who dread social situations often say that what bothers them most is the fear that they'll have nothing to say. This is an unfounded fear. Nobody cares what you have to say until they have learned to value you. So don't concentrate on a skill you don't need to have. All you need, in most social and business situations, is the capacity to ask questions. Asking questions is a great way to build relationships. Questions get other people talking. People like to talk. The problem is that the world has a constant imbalance between those who want to talk (the majority) and those who want to ask questions (the minority). Everybody has friends, or perhaps the better word might be 'acquaintances', who talk about themselves all the time and show no interest in others. Whether you say, 'I was working on this last week,' or 'I saw so-and-so in town the other night,' they immediately leap in with their tales of being forced to work unreasonable hours or top your story with someone much more famous they spotted. If you tell them you have a cold, they have flu. If you have flu, they have double pneumonia. No matter where any conversation starts, they wangle it so they get to talk about themselves constantly. I know someone, for example, who (clearly because they were trained to do so at some stage) asks the occasional question.

'How was work this week?' will be their query.

'Ah, great,' I'll say. 'You know, in the current meltdown, I can't get over the fact that we're doing OK. I'm working on some interesting projects.'

'Yeah, same here,' is the response and before I draw breath, he's into his saga of the week's intriguing travails. He never checks why I'd be interested. (I'm not.) He never works out how to make it interesting. (He could.) He's just talking, because it reassures him.

He has a problem shared by many people who are convinced that because they ask questions, they're good listeners. It doesn't follow. Many people, when they listen, are listening-to-talk. Like my friend, what they're looking for in the other person's conversation is a hook on to which they can hang whatever they want to talk about.

We all do it at times without knowing we do it. But if you observe your own conversations, you may be shocked to find out just how often you are listening with half your mind, while the other half scurries about looking for an opportunity to take over the jammy job: the talking.

In the workplace, a great way to build relationships is to give time and listen to your colleagues. What's important is really to listen, not multi-task and give someone a portion of your attention. For example, when someone comes to your desk with a problem, stop doing what you're doing. Move away from your computer and give the person your full and undivided attention. (If what you're working on is urgent, tell them nicely that you'll be back to them in ten minutes because you need to get whatever it is off your desk asap.) When they've outlined the issue, don't start talking immediately. If you let a silence fall, or say, 'Go on,' nine times out of ten, you'll find that they really have something much deeper on their mind that they want to share.

Sometimes, just talking the problem out loud with someone prepared to give uninterrupted attention allows the other person to solve their problem, so you don't have to come up with a solution. You may not have a solution and it may not be what they're looking for. So just ask them how you can help; don't jump in with a solution. The free gift of your attention is often the best thing you can give to another human being. The oddity is that when you let someone else do all the talking, they tend to develop a sense of you as being very interesting and will certainly walk away with a positive impression of you.

Learning to ask questions and to listen respectfully and attentively is a greatly underestimated double-sided life-skill. It's a life-skill that you can teach yourself and if, for example, you've been laid off and have a little time on your hands, now's the time to start to train yourself to interview in a way that will be vital with (future) clients and colleagues. You should learn to ask open questions.

'Do you like sun holidays?' is a closed question. It allows only two answers: yes or no.

'What kind of holidays do you like?' is an open question. It allows a vast range of answers.

'Do you play hurling?' is a closed question.

'What sports do you play?' is an open question.

A good rule of thumb is that questions beginning with 'Do you' tend to be closed, whereas questions beginning with 'How' tend to be open.

- Learn to ask appreciative questions: 'How did you manage that with all those difficulties?'
- Learn to probe further: 'Tell me a little bit more about that,' or, 'Why did you decide that?'
- Learn to ask directive questions: 'Talk to me about...' or, 'Go on.'
- Learn to ask questions without saying anything, with a smile, the raise of an eyebrow.

Learning to ask questions rather than fill the air with small talk has enormous advantages, if you concentrate on doing your damnedest to find out interesting stuff about and from every person you meet. The first advantage is that people, when the warm light of someone else's attention is shone on them, tend to become much more interesting than they appeared at first glance.

The second advantage is that you make links. Ireland is a small country and if you pay attention and ask the right sort of questions, you'll sooner or later find out that you and the other person share a relative, a mutual friend or a favourite place.

The third advantage is that you learn from the other person. You learn ways of tackling problems; you learn how a business or a sport works. You hoover up material that, stored away, will sooner or later become useful to you.

Finally, you create trust. You build, rather than unbuild a relationship. Sharing an office with the chairman of my company, Tom Savage, I've been fascinated to overhear phone calls from people to him which clearly establish that they met him only once, quite a while back, but believe they have a relationship with him and can trust him. What's even more fascinating is how often Tom remembers them and quotes back something they said to him during their earlier meeting.

Tom has an amazing memory. Not everybody has the habit of mind of storing material that emerges in a casual conversation, even if it's the focused conversation you have with a friend, a client, a colleague, when you have asked yourself, 'What makes this person different?' If you don't have a good memory, there's no harm in writing down what you learn about a person, because it may allow you to do, with a little electronic help, what Tom Savage can do on his own: remember key things about individuals you meet and use the material when you meet them again. There's no virtue in saying, 'Oh, it would be artificial to take notes to remind me that her husband's name is Mick.' It would be effortful to make that note, but the fact that you can ask how their husband Mick is doing, at some later point, registers for them the attention you paid to them. It makes them feel good. What's artificial about taking the time and making the effort to do that? We must never flatter ourselves that inattention to other people is somehow more authentic than making the effort to pay attention to them and find them interesting. Just because something is easy and natural doesn't make it right. As film star (she played Princess Leah in Star Wars), writer and recovering alcoholic Carrie Fisher found out. In *Wishful Drinking*, the book based on her one-woman show, Fisher remembers attending a three-hour Alcoholics Anonymous meeting.

> I heard someone say that I didn't have to like meetings, I just had to go to them. Well, this was a revelation to me! I thought I had to like everything I did. And for me to like everything I did meant – well, among other things, that I needed to take a boat-load of dope. Which I did for many, many years. But if what this person told me were true, then I didn't have to actually be comfortable all the time. If I could, in fact, learn to experience a quota of discomfort, it would be awful news. And if I could consistently go to that three-hour meeting, I could also exercise and I could write. In short, I could actually be responsible.

Carrie Fisher was gobsmacked by the fact that some of the best things we can do for ourselves may seem like an awful pain in the neck at the time. Like paying attention when being introduced to a line-up of people. Like asking questions of individuals we're sure are not half as interesting as we are. Like listening to the answers.

Names, as you'll find reiterated throughout this book, give you an insight into the person's history, background, beliefs. Each and every one of us has our name hard-wired into us. For example, people who suffer from Alzheimer's rarely forget their own name. In intensive care units around the world people are having their name shouted at them, because if someone will react to anything, it'll be their name. Names are vital. And I don't believe people who say they're bad with names. They're just lazy. We believe that what we do in the Communications Clinic is different. One of the first thing course participants notice is the lack of name badges on our courses. We never use name badges. We believe that name badges automatically damage the relationship with people, because instead of concentrating on them and learning who they really are, your concentration is half on the easy prompt of the name badge. It's a free pass to ignoring the other person or paying them just a bit more than cursory attention. Sometimes on our courses we have a room with twenty participants and it is our job to learn each and every one of those names.

Yet, as you could confirm from your own experience, name recall at social functions tends to be low. I'm sure it has happened to you: you're chatting to someone, a friend comes to join you and when you go to introduce them, you can't remember the other fellow's name. This can be mortifying and it certainly does nothing for the relationship. The reason we lose names is that we don't catch them in the first place. When we're introduced, we're often so focused on ourselves that we don't quite hear the new name.

Rule 1: Make sure you hear each new name. And get it right.
If the room is noisy or you simply aren't sure what was said, be sure to clarify. 'Was it Marie or Mar*ie*?', 'Is it Caroline or Carolyn?' (My fiancée's name is Carolyn. At this stage

Carolyn has given up correcting people when they call her Caroline. She claims she doesn't mind but she notices when someone gets it right.)

Rule 2: Use the name immediately but don't overuse it.
'Nice to meet you, Marie,' or 'So tell me, Marie, how do you feel about Peter's recent promotion?' Don't overuse it. I had a client whom I had to tell to stop using my name so regularly. You may say that's harsh, but it was every thirty seconds and it got to the point where I had stopped listening to what he actually wanted me to hear, because I was so busy with internal bets with myself that he'd do it again in twenty-seven seconds.

Rule 3: Quote people by name.
'Sean, Ciara was saying that...' Watch out for the common names like John or Pat. You'll forget them. Unusual names are easier to remember. Ireland is a multicultural society now, so when you need a first name, ask for it. But ask for it as a first name. Asking someone for their Christian name is not recommended, especially if they're Muslim, Jewish or atheist.

Rule 4: Spell the name right
When you are writing to someone, whether it's a covering letter or an email, be sure to spell it right. My name can be spelt three ways – Owen, Eoin, Eoghan. If some sends me a letter with either of the first two, they're already on a downer.

When you're listening you need to be listening to differentiate and remember. In his book, *Information*

Anxiety, Richard Saul Wurman writes that human beings are bombarded with information and because of this find it difficult to see significance in it and remember it. We get more information in a copy of the Sunday edition of *The New York Times* than a mediaeval scholar would have encountered in a lifetime. Our ability to remember hasn't improved but our ability to edit has. When chatting with colleagues or meeting clients we can sometimes hear things but disregard them and forget them. Listening to differentiate means actively seeking to capture what is different about this client and their business. That means refusing to accept the obvious. A pay-off for you from listening to differentiate and remember is that the person becomes more interesting. On the flip side they find you more interesting. Good listening meets that essential human need to be found worth listening to.

I meet shy clients on a weekly basis, who hate talking about themselves, hate small talk and chat. When I tell them the best cure for shyness is interviewing, at first they don't believe me. Then they try it and I get an ecstatic phone call.

'You don't have to give anything about yourself away,' one desperately shy woman told me last week. 'It keeps the attention off yourself and you're learning about someone new. I actually enjoyed it.'

This particular client had been on social anxiety medication for over a year and had decided she had to learn ways of coping with a central aspect of her job: meeting people. Learning to ask questions and simply listen to understand rather than win or talk was a major breatkthrough for her, as it is for many socially uneasy people, because it always works. Always.

People find that they can listen superbly when they want to. That 'want to' usually comes from a desire to win an argument.

'I'm going to listen to every word this guy says because I'm gonna prove him wrong,' people think to themselves.

Listening with the objective of verbally trouncing someone else may give you satisfaction but it is useless in building relationships and communicating effectively. Effective listening is vital to relationships. And relationships are vital to your career development – your network, your colleagues and your clients. Listening applies, first of all, if you are selling, whether that be a product, a service or an idea. People buy from people. They buy from people they like, people they have a relationship with. So they are more likely to buy from someone who questions intelligently and listens attentively. But these are skills which have applications outside the sales-floor. If you can maintain good customer relationships, your career will flourish.

YOUR ABILITY TO PRESENT YOUR POINT OF VIEW EMPATHETICALLY

The key thing you need to remember is to think before you speak. Figure out what the receiver's motives, feelings and interests are, then tailor your communication according to that information. People talk about 'getting the message across'. I've never liked the phrase. That approach is internally focused (on you rather than on the passive recipient of your message) and focused on your messages. I'd prefer you to view communication as 'creating understanding'. Because simply transmitting a message, a slogan or an approach and hoping people will remember it is at the motor mechanics end of good communication. In order for you to create understanding in another mind, you need to know that other mind. Once you know the mind you want to influence, you are much more likely to package and illustrate what you want them to remember appropriately and empathetically. The more you do that, the more effective you will be. If you don't, you could be described as blunt and thoughtless...which is, of course, not great for your career.

YOUR ABILITY TO TRADE AND NEGOTIATE

In Chapter 9, which dealt with performance reviews and pay negotiations, we covered some of the key principles and elements of good negotiations. Effectively, all interactions are negotiations. All our communications are designed, ultimately, to change someone's behaviour in the interest of someone else.

Good negotiating in the workplace is also vital to your career and success. If, for example, one of your colleagues asks you to photocopy a document for them and your response is 'No,' well, when you ask them for a favour down the line, no matter how affable they are, they could be tempted to give you as much as you gave them – nothing. A lot of this is just being a good team player but these micro-negotiations don't go unnoticed by colleagues and bosses. A colleague who never helps out but is always looking for help will quickly become unpopular in the office and will meet resistance from their peers when they try to introduce new ideas (no matter how good the ideas are). The old cliché, 'I'll scratch your back and you'll scratch mine,' is a crude summary of human reciprocity.

This 'web of indebtedness' can make all the difference to how you get on in the office. A young man who had been on work experience in a company where I used to work made a proud announcement on his final day: 'I can honestly say I never made one cup of tea in the weeks I was here.'

I don't know what he thought he was proving, but what he was actually proving was that those of us who had tagged him an unhelpful waster in the first week of his work experience now felt totally justified in our views. If any future potential employer telephoned us to find out about our experience with him, I would tell them that he'd been most proud of the fact that he had never made any of us a cup of tea. I wouldn't need to say anything critical. Out of the mouths of babes and work experiencers… Oh, lest I forget to say it, if you're on work experience be prepared to do anything you are asked to do and better still, don't wait to be asked.

When it comes to clients your ability to create a web of influence and your capacity to negotiate and trade are crucial. It might be doing them a favour or giving them advice off the pay clock. These favours and helping hands don't go unnoticed. People will remember them. Giving more than you're paid for always strengthens the relationship.

YOUR ABILITY TO HANDLE CONFLICT AND/OR CRITICISM WHEN IT HAPPENS

Our first reaction to conflict or criticism is defensive. One of my colleagues was making a TV commercial one day close to an estate effectively guarded by two Rottweilers, who kept coming closer to the camera crew and barking in a threatening way. The rest of the crew retreated and wondered if the denim in their jeans was thick enough to withstand Rottweiler teeth – with the exception of the cameraman, who put down his camera and suddenly made a mad run at the two dogs, yelling and waving his arms. They took off like bullets. They had expected defensiveness, not full-frontal attack.

The Americans have a phrase for this reality. 'When you're defending,' they say, 'You're losing.'

If, the moment you're attacked or criticised, your reflexive response is to defend yourself, be consoled. You're with the majority. But it's still not the right place to be. You need to retrain yourself so that criticism becomes something you can learn from. The only way that can happen is if you ask for more rather than trying to turn the tap off. It may sound paradoxical but that's the way to go. When someone criticises you in a general way, ask for specific examples of the behaviour that bothers them. This approach helps both sides in the equation. It stops you from being creased by the criticism and allows you to behave as if you were a third party who needed help to improve their performance. And, at the same time, it damps down the other person's anger (if there is any) and impresses them with your openness.

Conflict is easy to deal with if you were brought up in a family that regarded shouting matches and slammed doors as normal parts of the overall relationship. It's hard to deal with if you didn't. Conflictual situations are best handled using two devices: questions and quiet. The questions are to find out precisely what's behind what often seems to be an irrational attack. The quietness is used to drain the hostility out of the encounter. If, when someone is in a towering rage and is shouting at you, you lower your voice and answer them calmly and quietly, you'll force them to lower their voice to match yours and in the process, make them less angry. A quiet voice is a great anger-draining mechanism. Try to take any conflict out of the area of emotion, feeling and personal perception and into the area of fact, data and deliverables.

The most important thing to remember, in any situation

involving anger, is that you can win a battle and lose a war. You can defeat someone who is angry and illogical but destroy a friendship in the process. Try to get the infuriated person away from other people, calm the tenor of the encounter and seek consensus, remembering at all times that whatever you do will help to build or unbuild the relationship.

11

CLOTHES AND APPEARANCE –
LOOKING THE PART

'You only get one opportunity to make a first impression.'

It's an awful cliché. And like most awful clichés, it has a grain of truth in it. In the case of the job-seeker, it has a lot more than a grain of truth in it.

People employ people who they think will do their company credit. If you arrive into the interview wearing ripped jeans and a T-Shirt, the interview panel doesn't think, 'He only looks like this at the weekends and probably has a wardrobe full of business suits that he'll wear as soon as we give him the job.' They think, 'He's a scruffy fellow.'

They also, perhaps subconsciously, feel that wearing this outfit is disrespectful to them, suggesting that you can't be bothered to scrub up for an interview *they* regard as extremely important.

Sometimes, job-seekers take the attitude that they are so patently the right person for the job that clothing and grooming are side-issues. Sometimes, job applicants get self-righteous about it and opine that the interviewers should be able to see past the peripherals and focus on the realities. Either is the wrong attitude to take and can do enormous damage to your chances of employment. You are putting an unnecessary speed-bump in the path of your own progress.

The bottom line is that you'd better be dressed and groomed to the nth degree when you go to a job interview. That doesn't include the old notion that women should wear gloves, removing one of them for the handshake. That's history. What's not history is the need to present the best of yourself at any interview, just as being in time is important, in the message it sends to a prospective employer. So is dressing as if you value the opportunity to lay out your wares for a future (you hope) employer.

The best pieces of advice my company always gives are simple. Not easy, but simple:

1. Dress how you'd like to be perceived.
2. Dress for the job that you want, not the job that you're in.

The first needs a little explanation. Many young women would like to be perceived as fashionable, good-looking and sexy. So when it comes to an interview, they opt for low-slung tops, fabrics that are more appropriate to social settings (like clingy Lycra and satin), overly short skirts, fishnet tights and four-inch heels. The men on the interview panel may fancy them. The women on the panel will hate them. And both genders are likely to decide against them for showing such lack of judgement.

In this area, let me quote two unexpected sources of good advice. The first is the Stephanie Plum series of novels by Janet Evanovich. They're riotously funny in the way they deal with Stephanie, a bounty hunter with a chaotic work and love life. Stephanie's best pal is a former hooker, Lula, who has opted for a different career path, but who continues to dress as if she hadn't made the change. When people meet her their jaws drop.

The other piece of advice from an unexpected source is a comment I heard one evening when watching a television programme favoured by my fiancée. (Because I watch so much sport, she occasionally gets to view one of those programmes about trend-setting women.)

A fashionista on this particular television programme came out with an aphorism every woman should take to heart when job-seeking. 'Cleavage or legs, never both,' she said. 'And at work? Neither.'

Even if you discover that the corporate culture of the organisation in question doesn't major on formal clothing, you will never lose by erring on the side of formality. It shows respect for a potential employer.

When you are deciding what to wear, don't forget the following *dos* and *don'ts*.

- Do ask for advice. And not from your mother or your partner. If possible try to ask someone who specialises in clothes. For men and women there are specialist tailors you can go to. Alternatively, all the big department stores have advisers. Explain what you want to achieve by wearing the clothes you are seeking to purchase and the chances are that you will get good advice from them.
- Do coordinate your outfit. Even though you may love a certain tie or handbag be sure it matches

the rest of the outfit and doesn't distract.

- Do underplay your clothes. You need to be remembered for what you are, not what you wore. I have heard of interview panels where, at the end of a long day of interviewing, the board members have referred to individuals encountered during the day as, 'Your man with the shocking tie,' and, 'Your wan with the canary-yellow dress.'

- Don't fiddle with cuffs or edges or jackets or jewellery during an interview. Get in, sit down at the back of the chair, do any arranging of your person that you need to and from then on forget your clothing.

- Don't wear distractions. Distractions are ties with crazy designs on them or jewellery that moves.

- Don't wear anything louder than yourself. Your clothes are background music. You're in the foreground. They must remember you, not your wardrobe.

- Don't wear clothing or bring props which are inappropriate for the job to which you aspire. Like the woman who failed to get a job with a national charity because she carried a handbag easily identified as costing roughly €3,000, wore those expensive shoes with the red soles (everyone on the interview board recognised the Christian Louboutins) and produced a Mont Blanc fountain pen when she wanted to make a note of something during the interview.

- Don't spend all your time worrying about clothes. A client once told me she had been agonising for days over which of two suits to wear to an interview. I had a look at them and told her to flip a coin and to get back to preparing for her interview.

- Clothes and appearance are important. Important in the same way wallpaper is important if you plan to hang a good painting on it. It should be clean, unobtrusive and without distracting bubbles, in order to serve as an appropriate background for the painting. Clothes and grooming, similarly, are background.

- Another thing to watch for is how you smell. BO is an obvious no-no, but too much perfume or aftershave can be overpowering. Also watch what you eat or drink the night before. Especially watch for garlic. I love garlic. I love it on my steak, with chicken, even with mushrooms. But I hate to encounter it when I'm interviewing someone. It comes at you like waves from the Atlantic. Except not as refreshing.

- Never drink the evening before an interview. I interviewed a man last year and after five minutes the room (a very large room I might add) absolutely stank of booze. Now the fellow may have been saying wonderful things but the fact that he came into the interview smelling of booze immediately put a large X by his name. Either he drinks heavily all the time, in which case nobody will want to employ him, or he was at a party the previous night and rated his enjoyment of the craic more highly than the job he was seeking. Or he was so nervous that he'd taken a shot before turning up. Any one of the three justifies a negative response on the part of the prospective employer.

INDUSTRY VIEW: BILLY DIXON

Billy Dixon is a clothes guru. He works with politicians and TV stars. Whenever my company wants to provide a client with in-depth understanding of the kind of clothes they should wear for particular situations, we organise a session with Billy.

Oddly – or perhaps not so oddly – Billy lectured on packaging for many years in university. He says:

> Packaging for product is an absolute science. There are no ifs or buts about this. We use colour to project messages on packages that draw the consumer's eye in and make them buy. For example if you take Evian water. Water is clear and not blue. Evian puts the water in a blue bottle and when it's sitting on a shelf it shouts out, 'This is cool.' The white on the label speaks of its purity.

Billy used to talk to his students about Coca-Cola, using the colour red because red draws the eye so strongly that when you stack a lot of Coca-Cola tins on top of each other the human eye cannot ignore them.

But we're talking about people here, not cans or bottles. So how different is it with human beings? Not that different, in Billy Dixon's view. What you're doing is packaging a product.

> I don't look at it as a person. You're packaging the product and branding the product and trying to send out signals. First of all you always have to be appropriate. No matter how you dress it has to be appropriate. In terms of job interviews, the key thing is that men and women should always go in with structured clothing. This will normally come in the form of a jacket of some description, married with a pair of trousers or a skirt.

Every colour has a psychological profile. Billy Dixon maintains that darker colours like navy and grey have always made statements about their wearers that indicate authority. White, on the other hand, he sees as a very difficult colour for most men to wear.

> Unless a guy has very dark hair and tans easily, it just makes him look grey.

Billy, who has done a lot of work with politicians, says that viewers tend to be influenced by colours worn by politicians in their interpretation of those politicians' leadership capacity. Red is a leadership and power colour, so is frequently worn by US presidents and British prime ministers.

> Blue ties say 'safe and dependable' and that's what the President George W. Bush and Prime Minister Tony Blair partnership wore when they were

announcing the Iraq war. They refused to wear red ties, which are aggressive. They came out in blue ties to underline that it was really a peaceful thing they were doing. Bill Clinton was very fond of yellow ties because yellow is an energetic colour. In the 2007 Irish general election, Enda and Bertie both wore gold ties. What they were saying was, 'We are people of quality and depth.'

In an interview situation, depending on the job you're going for, Billy advises male interviewees to avoid red ties and white shirts.

If you have the dark suit, giving authority, the white shirt says 'cold' and the red tie says 'aggressive.' So you look as if you have lots of authority but you are unapproachable and very aggressive. In an interview situation it may only be a small point but it may make a difference in how you're perceived by the interview panel. For example if you had a female interviewer who was tuned into this, it could be detrimental to your chances.

Billy Dixon advises applicants to dress as they expect to have to dress in the job for which they're applying, and stresses that the imperative to wear the right clothes doesn't end when you get appointed.

Once you're in an organisation start taking a look at the influencers. These are people who make the decisions about your career. What way do they dress? Do they dress casually or formally? What is their approach? Mirror that. You have to adopt the mindset of the people who make the decisions.

12

EMPLOYMENT LAW – KNOWING YOUR RIGHTS

Tax and PRSI are not the only things that happen to you when you get a job. Any job brings with it certain rights and obligations. For you. And for your employer.

It's worth knowing about these for two reasons. Some of your rights will affect you immediately and you should be aware of them from day one. Secondly, if you do ever face redundancy or dismissal, or if you have other problems at work, you'll be in a far stronger position if you know your rights. Not that you'll necessarily have to be confrontational, let alone take things to a solicitor or the National Employment Rights Authority (NERA), but knowing what you're entitled to places you in a far better position.

Melanie Crowley, a partner with Mason, Hayes and Curran who specialises in employment law, predicts that employment law will become a lot more important for people:

> My work can be very cyclical. Over the last number
> of years when things were good, everyone was happy
> in their jobs, being well paid and with very little
> conflict. I spent a lot of time drafting contracts,

policies and procedures and working on bonus and incentive schemes. Now, with the way things are in the economy, with people losing their jobs and being made redundant with a much lower expectation of finding suitable alternative employment, I expect to see contentious employment issues go through the roof. I think employers will spend much more time in court defending their actions and I think, now more than ever, employees need to know their employment rights and their obligations.

If you're starting out in a job, have lost a job or think you are in danger of losing your job, this chapter is important to read. It is designed to give you a basic outline of the various rights that attach to your work. I've avoided going into the legal small print, so if you have a serious problem, or you feel you need more detailed information, please check out the website of NERA – www.employmentrights.ie – or the Department of Enterprise Trade and Employment's website – http://www.entemp.ie/sitemap/employmentrights.htm. The other possibility is to check with a solicitor. A first consultation is usually free, but be sure to check first; otherwise you could be landed with a hefty bill for what might seem like advice 'off the top of the head' given in only a few minutes.

The first thing to make is sure of is that you know your rights and your obligations. There is a number of ways to ensure you get your rights. If you believe you're not receiving one or more of your employment rights, as a first step you should always bring the issue to the attention of your employer. They may not be aware that they are required to provide you with a particular entitlement. By bringing the matter to their attention you may find that the issue can be resolved, rather than just complaining loudly about not getting your rights and damaging the relationship.

According to Melanie Crowley, many employees do not know their way around their employer's internal policies and procedures:

> An aggrieved employee shouldn't be running off to a solicitor or running to the Labour Court or the Employment Appeals Tribunal if they've got a grievance or a complaint to make, or they feel they are being bullied or harassed. In the first instance, they should look to their employer for the company's grievance procedure, which is effectively a complaints procedure. The complaint could be anything from not getting holidays, not getting a bonus or a spat with a colleague. Similarly there should be a bullying and harassment policy and procedure in place to deal with complaints of bullying and harassment. All policies and procedures should be employee-friendly and there should be assistance within an organisation to help an employee navigate their way around the policies should the need arise. The courts and the Employment Appeals Tribunal are increasingly saying, 'Look guys, you can't say you're miffed about something and then resign or say that you've been constructively dismissed unless you have tried to resolve the matter internally first. You have to give your employer a chance to address your complaint – whatever it relates to. If your employer doesn't

know about your complaint because you haven't told him, you can't expect him to be divinely inspired.'

If you're a member of a trade union, you could seek advice from your shop steward or relevant full-time union official in relation to your employment rights and entitlements and the options you have to seek to have them enforced. Complaints in relation to such rights as the minimum wage, working hours and carer's leave can be made to the Rights Commissioner Service. If you have a complaint about minimum notice and redundancy, it can be made to the Employment Appeals Tribunal.

You should also know your obligations. These aren't just in your contract of employment but obligations that stem from common law. For example, you have a duty not to breach the trust and confidentiality of an employer, which duty is, of course, reciprocal.

Another essential thing is to know your market. If, for instance, you're an auctioneer, you have to keep in mind that if you get dismissed or made redundant the chances of your getting another job in this area for the foreseeable future are slim. So you need to be as facilitative as possible with your employer. If they need to amend terms and conditions, agree. Because if they have to and you don't agree, the chances are you'll be made redundant and you won't get another job.

You need to look at what's going on in the world outside. It doesn't matter whether you're a pharmacist or a lawyer or a machine operator, you need to know that if something goes wrong you can get a job tomorrow or next week or in six months' time.

169

Not a lot of people know this but there is a way that you and your colleagues can find out what is coming down the tracks in your organisation. In 2006, Ireland began implementing a piece of legislation called the Information and Consultation Act. This legislation states that, from March 2008, in any organisation with more than fifty employees, the employees can have an information and consultation forum with their employer. It's been a total damp squib because employees haven't done anything about it. Nothing was done because the job market has been so great over the last couple of years. Things change.

The Information and Consultation Act stipulates that 10 per cent of employees (not less than fifteen or more than a hundred employees) should mobilise, go to the employer and say they want to set up an information and consultation forum. This can happen in any kind of organisation or company. It's nothing to do with a trade union and can happen whether or not the staff is unionised.

Once the staff has made the request, the employer has to consult with them on areas like potential restructurings, potential mergers, potential acquisitions and potential redundancies. This means that you and your colleagues would at least know a bit in advance about things coming down the tracks that could affect your working conditions and the security of your job.

REDUNDANCY
A contract of employment is terminated because of redundancy in a number of circumstances such as the following:

- where the employer's business or place of employment has partially or completely closed down
- where there has been a decrease in the employer's requirements for the category of qualification of the employees made redundant
- where fewer employees are required due to a restructuring or reorganisation of the business or because there has been a downturn in trade
- where the employer has decided that the work for which the employee had been employed should henceforth be done in a different manner for which the employee is not sufficiently qualified or trained
- where the employer has decided that a person who is also capable of doing other work for which the employee in question is not sufficiently qualified or trained should henceforward do the work

Any employee aged sixteen or over with two years' continuous service with an employer is entitled to a statutory redundancy payment in this situation. The statutory redundancy payment is two week's gross pay per year of service up to a ceiling of €600 per week plus one week's pay, which is also subject to the ceiling of €600. This payment is tax-free.

If you want more information about redundancy check out the website of the Department of Enterprise, Trade and Employment, www.entemp.ie. If the need arises you can calculate your entitlements with their redundancy calculator.

According to Melanie Crowley, the most important thing for both employees and employers to remember is that redundancies are all about a position, not about a person:

> If an employer has, for example, three account executives in his finance team and needs to reduce the head count by two, the employer must look, in the first instance, at the pool of employees who are potentially going to be affected by the reduction. The employer should then develop a set selection criteria in order to decide who goes. These selection criteria must be objective and fair. The (objective) selection criteria will usually focus on skills, qualifications, experience, flexibility and adaptability, but can extend, for example, to the cost of each individual and in some cases the performance or attendance records of each person.
>
> In order to make the redundancy process fair, employees should be involved at all stages and, at the very least, be given an opportunity to respond to and/or comment on the selection criteria and any 'scores' or weightings given to them. Generally, all things being equal and the employees equally qualified and all good performers, the criterion that's applied is 'last in, first out'. However, this is only a fall-back position and certainly not the only criterion for deciding who to make redundant. In circumstances where cost is a criterion, more expensive employees should be offered the

opportunity to work for a reduced amount as an alternative to being selected for redundancy. In the current climate, I expect this is something to which employees will increasingly agree.

13

DIFFERENT PATHS – CASE STUDIES

Over the last couple of years I've had the opportunity to meet people whose careers have changed more than they could ever have expected at the outset. The three factors that contributed to their success are always the same: hard work, ambition and luck.

I hate to go against Cardinal Newman, but the idea of a university has changed utterly since he wrote about it. The reality, today, is that few students have the financial freedom to have a great time studying their original course and then go on to several other disciplines, so that they achieve more than one master's degree and possibly a doctorate before taking the first step towards the career they eventually realise they want. Times are getting tougher and fewer graduates are going to have the time or money to go academically walkabout in that way in years to come.

That doesn't mean I'm suggesting that the course you choose when you leave school will determine the rest of your life – chances are it won't. Generation Y people (those born between 1980 and 1995), will change career (not just job) more readily than any previous generation. Your initial degree will open the first door but later on, doors will be opened by your experience in the workplace combined with your communication skills. The important factor is to get into the workplace early on and take further education while you work.

Don't buy into the idea that there's some impregnably logical, sure-fire way to ensure – right now – that you will pick the perfect course. There isn't. By the time you finish whatever you choose to study, you'll be a different person from the one you are now – with different dreams, hopes and potential. It's important to have something to aim for but third level choices don't come with a guarantee. Choices for the future never do.

Here are some examples of successful people who found themselves working in areas to which their initial choices in education would never have been expected to lead.

FERGUS FINLAY, CEO OF BARNARDOS
When you sat your Leaving Cert what did you have in mind?
Nothing, really. I had a vague idea that I wanted to do Law. I did my Leaving Cert in 1967 and in those days two honours would get you into college and four would get you a grant, so it wasn't hugely demanding getting into university. My aim was to get in and broadly speaking to do law.

So you got that?
I got into university but I didn't do law. I can't remember why I didn't. I did economics instead. My ambition in those days – believe it or not – was to be a trade union official.

Why?
Big Jim Larkin was my hero. What directed me down that

road was a book by Emmet Larkin about his father, Big Jim. That had a profound impact on me and I found the minute I read it I knew that's what I wanted to do. It helped me to form the core of beliefs and values that I've always had.

So why economics?
I thought if I had a grounding in public administration and economics it would be of some help. As it turned out it really wasn't. I became a trade union official immediately after leaving college but I couldn't honestly say that economics ever stood me in any stead at all. I think four years in college did help though – the discipline you learn, the ability to ask questions and the bit of confidence you develop all stood to me more than my degree.

You got your ambition, but didn't stay with it...
For the first twelve or fifteen years I did, then I got into politics by accident and worked as a political adviser for more or less the next twenty years. I went to work for Dick Spring for a year. I was commuting from Cork to Dublin and it was not intended to last. But there was never a good time to leave. Working with Dick and the Labour Party was hugely exciting. It became the centre of my life really.

How did you move from politics to Barnardos?
I had worked with Barnardos on a voluntary basis for a number of years. I was coming to the end of my time in politics and when the opportunity to work in an area that I thought was very important came along, I jumped at it. And I'd recommend that for anyone.

What do you mean?

People should do something they believe in. They should enjoy their job. Get fun out of their work. Be able to go to work wearing a smile. They should remember that money isn't everything. There is nothing quite as soul-destroying as a job you don't enjoy.

IVAN YATES OF CELTIC BOOKMAKERS

Did your Leaving Cert have any impact on what you're doing at the minute?

I'm remarkable in the fact that I didn't sit the Leaving Cert. I was boarding in one of the most expensive private schools in the country, St Columba's College in Rathfarnham, and getting on fine academically. But then what happened was that my father became terminally ill and he was very anxious that I return home to the family business. I spent a year in agricultural college and I ended up not sitting exams there either. I've no regrets about that though.

Why?

When you leave the formal education system at sixteen you become very focused. Every day of your adult life you need to compensate for not having a degree by having a really strong appetite for learning and that is what I have. Every day I learn something new. I'm very keen to learn from the brightest and the best, be it in politics, in business, in the media. I've never lost and hope never to lose that hunger for learning. And I wouldn't rule out going back to studying.

How did you get into politics?

My family had no background in politics and I actually had to look up the *Yellow Pages* to find out how to join Fine Gael. I was very lucky that I got a series of good breaks. Having been elected to the local council, I was then elected to the Dáil, aged twenty-one, at my first attempt. Learning the ropes of the local council, how to be a TD, how to be re-elected, how to get on to the front bench and how to be a minister was all very interesting, exciting and educational.

Why get out?
I had spent over twenty years in it and in 2001 I decided to leave. I was in my early forties had four kids, business opportunities and different interests. The novelty had worn off. I could see Fine Gael spending time in opposition and I knew I would find that very frustrating.

When did you become a bookie?
I did it as a hobby because I was a punter myself. I opened my first shop in Tramore in December 1987 purely as an adventure and not with any particular prospect of making money. I made every conceivable mistake but I learned from them. When I left politics in 2001 Celtic Bookmakers had sixteen shops; today we have sixty-four and a turnover of somewhere between €180 and €200 million. We employ more than three hundred people and we're one of the largest independent bookmakers.

What advice would you give someone starting off their career?
Well, success is 99 per cent perspiration and 1 per cent inspiration, with extra determination thrown in. You should never stop learning or listening. The world doesn't owe you a living. Don't have a chip on your shoulder. Learn from your

mistakes. Don't forget the little things:

- Your word is your bond.
- It's nice to be nice.
- Flattery gets you everywhere.
- And live to work rather than work to live.

ROSS DUFFY, IRISH HEAD OF MÉDECINS SANS FRONTIÈRES

In school could you see yourself working in aid?
I hoped I would be. I'd have been very surprised if you told me at eighteen that I was going to work in Iraq, the Congo or Pakistan. I went to school with the Holy Ghost Fathers in Blackrock in Dublin and they've a strong missionary tradition there. I was very fortunate to hear some fantastic speakers in school. I remember two people who escaped the atrocities in East Timor came in to us. They spoke about the horrific things they'd witnessed, the family and friends they'd seen brutally killed in front of them. It was deeply affecting and I was very moved by it. I had the compulsion to do something and that has stayed with me.

Did you study anything aid-related in college?
No. I studied BESS (Business, Economics and Social Studies) in Trinity and to be honest it wasn't a good fit with me. It didn't float my boat. It was a very general course. But I wanted to study in Trinity. There was a strong trend in South County Dublin schools to go to UCD and I wanted to get away from that and to start meeting new people.

Did you do any work experience during college?

I used my summers to develop my interests and explore different avenues: the London Stock Exchange, sailing, overseas aid. When I felt brave enough I volunteered in Uganda with Voluntary Service Ireland. They send students overseas for short placements. It was a fantastic opportunity to see what aid work was all about, to see if I would be good at it and if I had skills to offer. That's where I stumbled upon MSF. They were providing medical aid to refugees and victims of violence on the Congo border. I spent three years developing my skills to get into MSF as a logistician. I did courses and voluntary work, all to build my awareness and understanding so that I had something to offer them. After all that I found myself working with them as a logistician in the Congo, taking care of logistics, organising the supply chain and getting the drugs to the right place. And it's a job I'm very proud of.

SEÁN ÓG Ó HAILPÍN, CORK HURLING STAR AND COMMERCIAL MANAGER WITH ULSTER BANK

Were you happy with your Leaving Cert results?

I got about four hundred and twenty points and I was delighted because I had had massive hurling commitments. I wasn't expecting to do so well. I was playing with eleven, twelve, thirteen teams, so studying for the Leaving Cert was a tough job. My first choice was UCC and I didn't get that but I got enough points to study Fiontar in DCU (a business degree course delivered through the Irish language) so I took that. Then it dawned on me that I actually had to go up to Dublin.

How did that affect you?

I wasn't prepared for it. To be honest I was a small bit frightened. The only other option for me was repeat and there was no guarantee that I'd get UCC second time round. I viewed it as a bird in the hand is worth two in the bush. For me, going up to Dublin, it was either sink or swim. Over the four years away I developed as a person. I was a shy kid but going up to Dublin I decided to make a real go of it. I began to develop as an individual and it gave me a new network of friends that I wouldn't have had if I'd stayed in Cork. When I look back at my time in Dublin they were my best years. Getting away from Cork, away from home, gave me more independence and got me to grow up. I wouldn't be the person I am today if it wasn't for my years in Dublin and DCU.

Do your Leaving Cert and degree rate anywhere near your hurling successes for you?

I view my educational achievements more highly than my hurling accolades. I can only be at the top in sport for ten years and after that it's gone. Furthering my education gave me better prospects, opened more doors and gave me every chance of getting a good job. Hurling gave me a great work ethic, though, and the qualities I learned from sport I've applied in my work in Ulster Bank, like working in teams and hard work.

Did you always see yourself in a bank?

I knew I'd be in business in some way but not necessarily as a banker. When I went to DCU and Fiontar I studied finance, accountancy and other business subjects and during the summer I was lucky enough to get work experience in banks at home. When I finished my degree I'd been working in banks for the previous couple of summers and knew the way they operated and what they expected of me. These experiences taught me a commitment and an understanding that when you work for a large organisation they expect standards of behaviour and they mirrored the experience of the real job. Everything I've done so far has led me to this job – my studies, my hurling and my experience.

TERRY PRONE, DIRECTOR OF THE COMMUNI-CATIONS CLINIC
Do you remember the day you got your Leaving Cert results?
No. I remember the importance of the Leaving Cert, though. My parents said I had to go to university to get a degree I could fall back on if I didn't succeed in acting. I had been acting in the Abbey Theatre from the time I was sixteen. So I got a good Leaving Cert, went to UCD and lasted less than a year. I couldn't understand a word of the Philosophy course. About the only thing I got out of that year was marginally better spoken Irish. That mattered because the Abbey – back then – required its actors to sound like native speakers.

Were you happy in UCD for that year?
Hated every minute of it. Still have nightmares about it. I'm not a social person so I didn't join anything, I just attended. I escaped because an actor named Joan O'Hara, playing a major role in Boucicault's *The Shaughraun*, got pregnant. The Abbey were due to do the play in London precisely when she was due to have her baby. I was a great mimic – I could do the entire performance exactly the way Joan did it and it

was an obvious choice for the Abbey to have me step into the role. For me, it was the opportunity of a lifetime and I wasn't going to miss it even if – as it did – it clashed with the first year exams. Thank God. I never went back.

How did you end up in the communications business?
When I was thirteen I was sent by the Holy Faith nuns in my school to be in the audience of a TV programme called *Teen Talk*, presented by a man named Bunny Carr. It was a little bit like *Questions and Answers* only the audience were all teenagers. During the programme I got argumentative and stroppy and at the end Bunny called me out and said, 'I want you on the panel next week.' From then on he never lost sight of me. When he became director of the Catholic Communications Centre he rang me up and booked me to help a group of parish priests improve their sermons. That was the first communications consultancy I did, when I was about twenty. Everything in between led me to the position I have now: Director of the Communications Clinic.

You didn't have a career plan that brought you to this point?
I had a great career plan. I was going to be the greatest actress the Abbey had ever had. Running a business was never on the agenda, but, as it turned out, has been much more fun than I ever imagined. I have limited faith in career-planning, because of the number of weird changes that have happened to me. Every time I think I have things sorted it goes like the path in *Alice through the Looking Glass* and turns me back to the direction I'm coming from. Every career plan I ever had failed – and caused me to do something unplanned, completely different and a hell of a lot more interesting.

14

And Finally, Retirement

I decided to write about retirement because retirement is actually your last job and you should be preparing for it the way you prepared for your first job. It's a point of massive change in your life.

The whole concept of retirement is relatively recent. The German Chancellor Otto von Bismarck (1815–98) was the man who invented what we no longer call the Old Age Pension. In the years since Bismarck came up with a way of keeping older people from dying of starvation, the concept of retirement has greatly changed, not least because of the increasing life span (in Bismarck's day, life expectancy was forty-five). Sixty-five, just a century ago, was next door to death, assuming you lived that long in the first place. Sixty-five, these days, gives you two or three decades more and the statistics indicate that for most people, those decades can be healthy, active, contributory and fulfilling.

Just like a new job, retirement is going to bring you a whole new set of challenges and opportunities. And new colleagues, even if they are your husband, the dog and the geraniums. When you retire you face the fact that you probably have another twenty or so years of 'leisure'. You'll realise after the initial relief that it's a fair length of time and that you run the risk of becoming a little bored. You have to ask yourself what you want to do with the rest of your life? Many people who have not given this much thought before retiring find it very difficult. They sit there looking at the hour hand move slowly around the watch that they were presented with at the retirement party, not knowing what to do.

While you may not want to go back to the daily grind of a forty-hour week, you may find (a) that you don't have enough money put aside to cover your living expenses; (b) you're bored out of your mind; and (c) there are still things that you want to do. Many business people over sixty-five like to keep their hand in the game after they retire to keep themselves occupied and earn a few bob. In the US, they are preferred employees in many states, where employers rate experience and commitment highly. Increasingly, Irish employers think the same way. If you are in this situation you should figure out what it is that you'd like to do and how much time you want to devote to it. Even if you've left your old company, many good firms bring past employees back in part-time positions or as consultants. Other companies in the US have started running phased retirement programmes that allow a reduction in working hours over a period of years, made possible financially by provision of a partial pension.

The baby boomers and people on the cusp of retirement will change the face, the image and definition of retirement. For many, retirement will no longer signal the end of working, but rather a career and lifestyle change, where the retiree has multiple options – such as continuing to work (though perhaps at a different pace), returning to college for additional training or education, changing careers, venturing

185

into entrepreneurship, becoming more involved in volunteer work or simply enjoying leisure and travel possibilities – a mix of working, learning, relaxing and trying new things.

People on the brink of retirement can suffer the same confusion about themselves and their life as a pubescent teenager, especially for those whose identity for forty years or more has been bound up with their job. But it is a time for growth and reinvention. Long before it happens, when you see retirement coming into focus you should start envisaging your future, ideally by attending a pre-retirement planning course. The Catholic Church refuses to marry couples who haven't attended a pre-marriage course. It's arguable that some of the same emphasis should be put on pre-retirement planning courses.

John Higgins, CEO of the Retirement Planning Council of Ireland (providers of pre-retirement courses), believes that there are lots of myths about retirement and that the big thing people need to remember is that healthy relationships are the key:

> There are all these things that we neglect even to take heed of in relationships and relationships to me are the core of a happy retirement. Planning for retirement is so important. What we flag for people is that health is primary. We set out to lessen the myths surrounding retirement and there's an awful lot of myths, many about money. We find that money has dropped way down the list of what people facing retirement are worrying about. By the time they meet us they know that they have to have a healthy

lifestyle but the thing they often forget about is relationships.

While you're working, your network is made up of 20 per cent family and friends and 80 per cent work colleagues or people you meet through work. The question we ask is: who is going to replace the 80 per cent you will lose when you retire? And what we say is join, join, join.

The other thing to remember is that whereas you used to come home at six or seven o'clock and have a few hours with your family, when you retire it becomes 24/7 at home. You and your partner are occupying the same home, so you need to make sure that there is compromise and agreement in order to have a harmonious relationship. People bring bad habits from work – habits which are fine at work but not at home. For example they presume that they can just set up meetings because that is what they are used to at work but they forget to tell the other person with whom they share their home.

We get people to draw up a list of hobbies and then say, 'Here are two hundred possible hobbies. You should have at least one that you have a passion about – golf or whatever it is. You should also think about doing something different every year. For example if you were someone who never cooked an egg in his life, maybe do a cookery course this year. Next year it could be jet skiing.'

15

Go for It

Getting the right job is never easy. Getting the right job in a recession is desperately hard. As this book goes to print, we're seeing photographs of queues where as many as two thousand people have lined up to be interviewed for perhaps a hundred jobs. That's tough. But that's the reality.

Your capacity to build a worthwhile career depends on three things:

- How you cope with negative circumstances
- How you motivate yourself and others
- How you constantly assess how you're doing

If you find yourself always focused on the difficulties of your situation, you need to force yourself into 'realistic optimism'. Realistic optimism is the kind that says, 'This is going to take perhaps fourteen months longer than I'd like, but at the end of the process, what I learn during every one of those fourteen months will have made me a better executive/ teacher/consultant.'

One of my recurring pieces of advice to people like you who are looking for jobs is that you should maintain your own optimism by hanging around with people who make you more, rather than less, buoyant. People who make you laugh. You don't have to share all your bad news with those people. In fact, I'd suggest that one of the bits of information you never share is the humiliation of applying for a post or being interviewed for a position, and failing to get even the basic courtesy of a reply afterwards. It's not fair. It's not acceptable. But you know what? It's a reality. It affects everybody who's currently on the job-hunt. Get over it and keep quiet about it. On the other hand, whenever you get a muted positive – like, for example, a HR manager coming back to you saying you were number two in the list rather than number one, keep in contact with that person. You can drop them a note of thanks and ask their advice; the chances are that if they have a temporary position to be filled, they'll think of the number two who had the wit not to sulk in silence.

Assessing how you're doing while you're doing it is one of the skills you must develop if you plan to have a serious career. For example, it should never happen that, a few months after you're appointed to your dream position and just as you're coming up to the end of your probation period, your manager calls you in and tells you she knows you understand that this is not working. If this happens and is a complete shock to you, you haven't been observing yourself ruthlessly enough.

During the job-seeking process, you face the same threats as every job seeker. The threat of tiredness. Tiredness, not just reflected in your face, but in the way your clothes hang. Tiredness that amounts to being defeated before the battle has begun. Think of yourself as a third party and take care of yourself just as you would take care of a friend going through difficult times.

And – finally – remember the great sports technique. Great athletes have always visualised the race they have to run or the fight they have to fight before they go through it. It is a powerful technique because it allows you to rehearse, face the worst and get through it – and do it all in your head before you have to do it in reality.

Then go for it.

Selected Bibliography

Crosbie, Alan. *Don't Leave It to the Children*. Dublin: Marino Books, 2002.

Fisher, Carrie. *Wishful Drinking*. New York: Simon and Schuster, 2008.

Persaud, Raj. *Staying Sane*. London: Bantam Press, 2001.

Seligman, Dr Martin. *Learned Optimism: How to Change Your Mind and Your Life*. New York: Pocket Books, 1992.

Maltz, Maxwell. *Psycho Cybernetics*. New York: Pocket Books, 1969.

Wurman, Richard Saul. *Information Anxiety*. New York: Doubleday, 1989.

Goleman, Daniel. *Emotional Intelligence*. London: Bantam Press, 1995.

Tufte, Edward. *The Cognitive Style of PowerPoint*. Cheshire, Connecticut: Graphics Press, 2003.